The Management and Financing of Colleges

A statement on national policy
by the Research and Policy Committee
of the Committee for Economic Development
October 1973

Library of Congress Catalog Card Number: 73-86038
International Standard Book Number: 0-87186-052-X
Design: Harry Carter
First printing: October 1973
Printed in the United States of America

Single copy: $1.50

Committee for Economic Development
477 Madison Avenue, New York, N.Y. 10022

Contents

FOREWORD: THE "WHY" OF THIS STATEMENT 7

1 INTRODUCTION AND SUMMARY OF RECOMMENDATIONS 9
   A Two-Part Strategy   14
   Diversity and Quality   16
   Better Management of Resources   17
   Goals and Funding Patterns   19
   SUMMARY OF RECOMMENDATIONS   21

2 GOALS, OBJECTIVES, AND ACCOUNTABILITY 27
   Defining Goals and Setting Objectives   28
   Effective Educational Planning   31
   Evaluation and Accountability   32

3 MANAGEMENT RESPONSIBILITY AND AUTHORITY 35
   The Trustees and Reserved Powers   36
   State Systems   38
   The President   39
   The Faculty   41
   The Students   43

4 MANAGEMENT AND EDUCATIONAL POLICY 45
   Management Methods and Personnel   46
   Planning and Budgeting   48
   Management and the Improvement of Teaching   49
   Nontraditional Education   50
   Strategies for Economy   52

5 ACADEMIC FREEDOM, JOB SECURITY, AND DUE PROCESS 56
   Faculty Tenure   57
   Faculty Collective Bargaining   59
   Due Process on the Campus   60

6 A STRATEGY FOR BETTER-TARGETED AND
  INCREASED FINANCIAL SUPPORT 62
   Equalizing Opportunity by Grants to Students   64
   Enlarging the Student-Loan Program   67
   Raising Low Tuition and Fees   68
   Effects of Increasing Support Through
      Student Grants and Higher Tuition   69
   Relating Institutional Support to Social Goals   71
   Strengthening Voluntary Support of Higher Education   74
   Annex: The Funding of Undergraduate Education   75

MEMORANDA OF COMMENT, RESERVATION, OR DISSENT 85

APPENDIX: RESEARCH PAPERS ON THE MANAGEMENT
              AND FINANCING OF COLLEGES 93

The Responsibility for CED Statements on National Policy

This statement has been approved for publication as a statement of the Research and Policy Committee by the members of that Committee and its drafting subcommittee, subject to individual dissents or reservations noted herein. *The trustees who are responsible for this statement are listed on pages 5 and 6. Company associations are included for identification only; the companies do not share in the responsibility borne by the individuals.*

The Research and Policy Committee is directed by CED's bylaws to:

Initiate studies into the principles of business policy and of public policy which will foster the full contribution by industry and commerce to the attainment and maintenance of high and secure standards of living for people in all walks of life through maximum employment and high productivity in the domestic economy.

The bylaws emphasize that:

All research is to be thoroughly objective in character, and the approach in each instance is to be from the standpoint of the general welfare and not from that of any special political or economic group.

The Research and Policy Committee is composed of sixty trustees from among the two hundred business men and women and educators who comprise the Committee for Economic Development. It is aided by a Research Advisory Board of leading economists, a small permanent research staff, and by advisors chosen for their competence in the field being considered.

Each statement on national policy is preceded by discussions, meetings, and exchanges of memoranda, often stretching over many months. The research is undertaken by a subcommittee, with its advisors, and the full Research and Policy Committee participates in the drafting of findings and recommendations.

Except for the members of the Research and Policy Committee and the responsible subcommittee, the recommendations presented herein are not necessarily endorsed by other trustees or by the advisors, contributors, staff members, or others associated with CED.

The Research and Policy Committee offers these statements on national policy as an aid to clearer understanding of the steps to be taken in achieving sustained growth of the American economy. The Committee is not attempting to pass on any pending specific legislative proposals; its purpose is to urge careful consideration of the objectives set forth in the statement and of the best means of accomplishing those objectives.

Research and Policy Committee

Chairman
PHILIP M. KLUTZNICK
Chairman, Executive Committee
Urban Investment and Development Co.

Co-Chairman
MARVIN BOWER, Director
McKinsey & Company, Inc.

Vice Chairmen
HOWARD C. PETERSEN, Chairman — *National Economy*
The Fidelity Bank

JOHN L. BURNS, President — *Education and Social & Urban Development*
John L. Burns and Company

WILLIAM H. FRANKLIN, Chairman — *International Economy*
Caterpillar Tractor Co.

JOHN A. PERKINS — *Improvement of Management in Government*
Vice President-Administration
University of California, Berkeley

SANFORD S. ATWOOD, President
Emory University

JERVIS J. BABB
Wilmette, Illinois

JOSEPH W. BARR, Chairman
American Security and Trust Co.

HARRY HOOD BASSETT, Chairman
First National Bank of Miami

[1] JOSEPH L. BLOCK
Former Chairman
Inland Steel Company

MARVIN BOWER, Director
McKinsey & Company, Inc.

JOHN L. BURNS, President
John L. Burns and Company

FLETCHER L. BYROM, Chairman
Koppers Company, Inc.

RAFAEL CARRION, JR.
Chairman and President
Banco Popular de Puerto Rico

JOHN B. CAVE
Senior Vice President
White Weld & Co., Incorporated

[1] JOHN R. COLEMAN, President
Haverford College

EMILIO G. COLLADO
Executive Vice President
Exxon Corporation

ROBERT C. COSGROVE, Chairman
Green Giant Company

JOHN H. DANIELS, Chairman
Independent Bancorporation

W. D. EBERLE
Special Representative for Trade Negotiations
Executive Office of the President

RICHARD C. FENTON, President
Cooper Laboratories International, Inc.

E. B. FITZGERALD, Chairman
Cutler-Hammer, Inc.

MARION B. FOLSOM
Rochester, New York

JOHN M. FOX, President
H. P. Hood Inc.

DAVID L. FRANCIS, Chairman
Princess Coal Sales Company

WILLIAM H. FRANKLIN, Chairman
Caterpillar Tractor Co.

KERMIT GORDON, President
The Brookings Institution

JOHN D. GRAY, Chairman
Omark Industries, Inc.

TERRANCE HANOLD, President
The Pillsbury Company

JOHN D. HARPER, Chairman
Aluminum Company of America

H. J. HEINZ, II, Chairman
H. J. Heinz Company

GILBERT E. JONES
Senior Vice President
IBM Corporation

EDWARD R. KANE, President
E. I. du Pont de Nemours & Company

CHARLES KELLER, JR., President
Keller Construction Corporation

JAMES R. KENNEDY, Vice Chairman
Celanese Corporation

PHILIP M. KLUTZNICK
Chairman, Executive Committee
Urban Investment and Development Co.

RALPH LAZARUS, Chairman
Federated Department Stores, Inc.

FRANKLIN A. LINDSAY, President
Itek Corporation

OSCAR A. LUNDIN
Executive Vice President
General Motors Corporation

G. BARRON MALLORY
Jacobs Persinger & Parker

THOMAS B. McCABE
Chairman, Finance Committee
Scott Paper Company

GEORGE C. McGHEE
Washington, D.C.

ROBERT R. NATHAN, President
Robert R. Nathan Associates, Inc.

ALFRED C. NEAL, President
Committee for Economic Development

DONALD S. PERKINS, Chairman
Jewel Companies, Inc.

[1] JOHN A. PERKINS
Vice President-Administration
University of California, Berkeley

HOWARD C. PETERSEN, Chairman
The Fidelity Bank

[1] C. WREDE PETERSMEYER
Chairman and President
Corinthian Broadcasting Corporation

R. STEWART RAUCH, JR., Chairman
The Philadelphia Saving Fund Society

PHILIP D. REED
New York, New York

MELVIN J. ROBERTS, Chairman
Colorado National Bank of Denver

[1] WILLIAM M. ROTH
San Francisco, California

ROBERT B. SEMPLE, Chairman
BASF Wyandotte Corporation

WILLIAM C. STOLK, President
Government Research Corporation

ALEXANDER L. STOTT
Vice President and Comptroller
American Telephone & Telegraph Company

WAYNE E. THOMPSON
Senior Vice President
Dayton Hudson Corporation

[1] ROBERT C. WEAVER
Department of Urban Affairs
Hunter College

SIDNEY J. WEINBERG, JR., Partner
Goldman, Sachs & Co.

[1] HERMAN L. WEISS, Vice Chairman
General Electric Company

FRAZAR B. WILDE, Chairman Emeritus
Connecticut General Life Insurance Co.

WALTER W. WILSON, Partner
Morgan Stanley & Co.

[1] THEODORE O. YNTEMA
Department of Economics
Oakland University

---

1. Voted to approve the policy statement but submitted memoranda of comment, reservation, or dissent, or wished to be associated with memoranda of others. See pages 85 to 92.

Subcommittee on Management and Financing of Colleges

Chairman
W. D. EBERLE
Special Representative for Trade Negotiations
Executive Office of the President

Vice Chairman
MARVIN BOWER, Director
McKinsey & Company, Inc.

SANFORD S. ATWOOD, President
Emory University

JERVIS J. BABB
Wilmette, Illinois

GEORGE F. BENNETT, President
State Street Investment Corporation

1 CHARLES P. BOWEN, JR., Chairman
Booz, Allen & Hamilton Inc.

FLETCHER L. BYROM, Chairman
Koppers Company, Inc.

1 JOHN R. COLEMAN, President
Haverford College

CHARLES E. DUCOMMUN, President
Ducommun Incorporated

LAWRENCE E. FOURAKER
Dean, Graduate School of Business Administration, Harvard University

JOHN M. FOX, President
H. P. Hood Inc.

HUGH M. GLOSTER, President
Morehouse College

1 LINCOLN GORDON
Fellow, Woodrow Wilson International Center for Scholars

JOHN D. GRAY, Chairman
Omark Industries, Inc.

WILLIAM E. HARTMANN, Partner
Skidmore, Owings & Merrill

SAMUEL C. JOHNSON, Chairman
S. C. Johnson & Son, Inc.

HARRY W. KNIGHT, President
Hillsboro Associates, Inc.

WILLIAM F. MAY, Chairman
American Can Company

H. TALBOTT MEAD
Chairman, Finance Committee
The Mead Corporation

LOUIS W. MENK, Chairman
Burlington Northern, Inc.

1 JOHN A. PERKINS
Vice President—Administration
University of California, Berkeley

1 ELLERY SEDGWICK, JR., Chairman
Medusa Corporation

ANNA LORD STRAUSS
New York, New York

JAMES E. WEBB
Washington, D.C.

Nontrustee Members

JOHN CHANDLER, President
Salem College

JOSEPH COORS
Executive Vice President
Adolph Coors Company

JOHN J. CORSON, Chairman
Fry Consultants Incorporated

JAMES C. DOWNS, JR., Chairman
Real Estate Research Corporation

ALVIN C. EURICH, President
Academy for Educational Development

CURTISS E. FRANK
Chairman, Executive Committee
Council for Financial Aid to Education, Inc.

ASA S. KNOWLES, President
Northeastern University

CHARLES R. LONGSWORTH, President
Hampshire College

LELAND L. MEDSKER
Director, Center for Research and Development in Higher Education
University of California

WESLEY W. POSVAR, Chancellor
University of Pittsburgh

PAUL C. REINERT, S.J., President
St. Louis University

ABRAM L. SACHAR, Chancellor
Brandeis University

D. THOMAS TRIGG, President
The National Shawmut Bank of Boston

HAROLD M. WILLIAMS
Dean, Graduate School of Management
University of California

*Nontrustee members take part in all discussions on the statement but do not vote on it.

Project Director
STERLING M. McMURRIN
Dean, Graduate School
University of Utah

Assistant Project Director
CARL RIESER
Director of Publications
Committee for Economic Development

Advisors to the Subcommittee

ROY BLOUGH
Graduate School of Business
Columbia University

EARL C. BOLTON
Vice President, Institutional Management Division
Booz, Allen & Hamilton, Inc.

ALAN K. CAMPBELL
Dean, The Maxwell School of Citizenship and Public Affairs
Syracuse University

KURT M. HERTZFELD, Treasurer
Amherst College

LAWRENCE C. HOWARD
Graduate School of Public and International Affairs
University of Pittsburgh

CHARLES B. HUESTIS
Vice President for Business and Finance
Duke University

JOHN W. LEDERLE
Joseph B. Ely Professor of Government
University of Massachusetts

HENRY M. LEVIN, Associate Professor
School of Education
Stanford University

RENSIS LIKERT, Chairman
Rensis Likert Associates, Inc.

THOMAS R. McCONNELL
Center for Research and Development in Higher Education
University of California

DAVID S. MUNDEL
John F. Kennedy School of Government
Harvard University

CED Staff Advisors
ARNOLD H. PACKER
FRANK W. SCHIFF

Research Advisory Board

Chairman
CARL KAYSEN
Director, The Institute for Advanced Study

EDWARD C. BANFIELD
The Fels Center of Government
University of Pennsylvania

ALAN K. CAMPBELL
Dean, The Maxwell School of Citizenship and Public Affairs
Syracuse University

RONALD R. DAVENPORT
Dean, School of Law
Duquesne University

CHARLES P. KINDLEBERGER
Department of Economics and Social Science
Massachusetts Institute of Technology

JOSEPH S. NYE
Center for International Affairs
Harvard University

ARTHUR OKUN
The Brookings Institution

RAYMOND VERNON
Graduate School of Business Administration
Harvard University

HENRY C. WALLICH
Department of Economics
Yale University

MURRAY L. WEIDENBAUM
Department of Economics
Washington University

PAUL N. YLVISAKER
Dean, Graduate School of Education
Harvard University

Foreword
The "Why" of This Statement

The era of campus violence seems to have passed. Students are no longer locking up administrators, burning buildings, or engaging in strikes. But the crisis in higher education is not over. Many colleges and universities are in financial trouble. Many students are still dissatisfied with some aspects of higher education. Professional pride is not keeping faculty members from joining unions.

Society meanwhile is reassessing the relative value of a college education. There is skepticism because a college degree is no longer ready assurance of a job. There is also evidence of reordering the place of higher education in the scale of national priorities as legislators question expenditures for this purpose. Yet the public still regards colleges and universities as major instruments for improving the quality of life and for preserving the essential features of the kind of society it wants to have.

In these circumstances our Committee has developed this policy statement on how an important national institution might move toward a solution of its problems and serve the interests of society more effectively. We were encouraged in this effort by The Danforth Foundation and The Ford Foundation, which have provided a major part of the funds for our studies. We deeply appreciate this assistance.

The trustees of CED, although predominantly business men and women, also include in their membership a number of college presidents and others of high academic status. In preparing this statement, the Committee had the good fortune to secure advice and guidance from among this group as well as from other outstanding academic authorities. An examination of the listing of educational advisors who assisted us (pages 6 and 95) will give some appreciation of the caliber of thought on which we drew. Supplementary papers prepared by these and other experts are listed in the Appendix.

It is only fair to state that the trustees and their academic advisors were not always of the same mind when shaping policy and recommendations. In two major instances where such a difference occurred, this Committee duly and respectfully notes the dissent of certain of the nontrustee members and advisors of the Subcommittee and emphasizes its full responsibility under CED statutes for the views expressed in the statement (see page 70).

We want to acknowledge particularly the splendid leadership of the Subcommittee chairman, Ambassador William D. Eberle, the President's Special Representative for Trade Negotiations and a trustee of Stanford University. The project director was Dean Sterling M. McMurrin of the Graduate School of the University of Utah, former United States Commissioner of Education, whose credentials are confirmed by his fine work in this and related efforts. He was assisted by J. Boyer Jarvis, associate academic vice-president of the University of Utah, and Larry L. Leslie, research associate, Center for the Study of Higher Education, and chairman, Higher Education Program of Pennsylvania State University. Recognition should also be given to the important contribution made to our studies by the Task Force on Alternate Sources of College Funding under Harry W. Knight, chairman, and David S. Mundel of the John F. Kennedy School of Government at Harvard University, co-chairman and study director.

Philip M. Klutznick, *Chairman*
Marvin Bower, *Co-Chairman*
Research and Policy Committee

Chapter 1
Introduction
and Summary of Recommendations

This policy statement was occasioned by the increasingly precarious financial condition and outlook of American colleges and universities. In 1971, about 60 per cent of all private four-year colleges had actual deficits (i.e., expenditures exceeded incomes). At the same time, numerous major public institutions also incurred deficits. In 1972, the condition worsened. Most institutions have had to reduce their programs in order to correct or avoid deficits; some have disposed of parts of their campuses; others have closed.

When we inquired into the causes of the colleges' financial condition, we identified two closely linked major factors.

The topping-off of the boom in enrollment. In the 1960s, it was widely assumed that the opportunity for schooling leading to the baccalaureate degree should be open to everyone who could pursue it successfully. This contributed to unparalleled enrollment increases as colleges and universities attempted, by expanding facilities and staffs, to accomplish what had been expected of them. The recent slackening in enrollments has now left many colleges with student vacancies and heavy fixed annual expenditures that are difficult or impossible to meet (see Figure 1).

Rapidly rising costs exceeding the general rate of inflation. Between 1966 and 1969, the annual rate of increase in per student costs was 6 per cent. Of this, an average of only 3.4 per cent per year was due to general inflation. The present annual increase in per student costs, excluding inflation, is 3.3 per cent. This is largely attributable to the lack of major productivity improvements in higher education (see Figure 2). The labor-intensive character of education makes increases in productivity much more difficult to achieve in colleges and universities than in areas where mechanization and automation are possible.* This situation is not uncommon in the service sector of the economy. Important improvements have occurred in higher education, especially in matters of quality; but here assessment of gains is difficult and sometimes impossible. Where productivity can be quantified, however, virtually no increases have occurred in recent decades.[1]

1/June O'Neill, *Resource Use in Higher Education* (Berkeley: Carnegie Commission on Higher Education, 1971).

*See Memorandum by MR. THEODORE O. YNTEMA, page 85.

Figure 1. In the 1960s, degree-credit undergraduate enrollment more than doubled, from 3 million to more than 6.5 million, an 8 per cent increase compounded annually. Since 1970, the rate of increase has averaged about 5 per cent annually. Some slackening was indeed anticipated for the 1970s, but the drop-off in the growth rate of enrollments has turned out to be sharper than predicted. Undergraduate degree-credit enrollments in the fall of 1972 were about 7.3 million, only 100,000 greater than the previous fall. (Total degree-credit enrollments in higher education, including both graduate and undergraduate students, were estimated at 8.2 million in 1972.)

Many colleges actually have experienced unexpected declines, and the prospects continue to be uncertain. According to a survey of 109 major state university systems and campuses made in the spring of 1973 by the National Association of State Universities and Land-Grant Colleges, applications at public institutions decreased by 4.2 per cent overall, as compared with the figures in the spring of 1972. By contrast, Ivy League colleges showed a healthy increase for the second consecutive year.

Figure 1
Degree-Credit Enrollment in Institutions of Higher Education, 1959 to 1972 *(fall of year)*

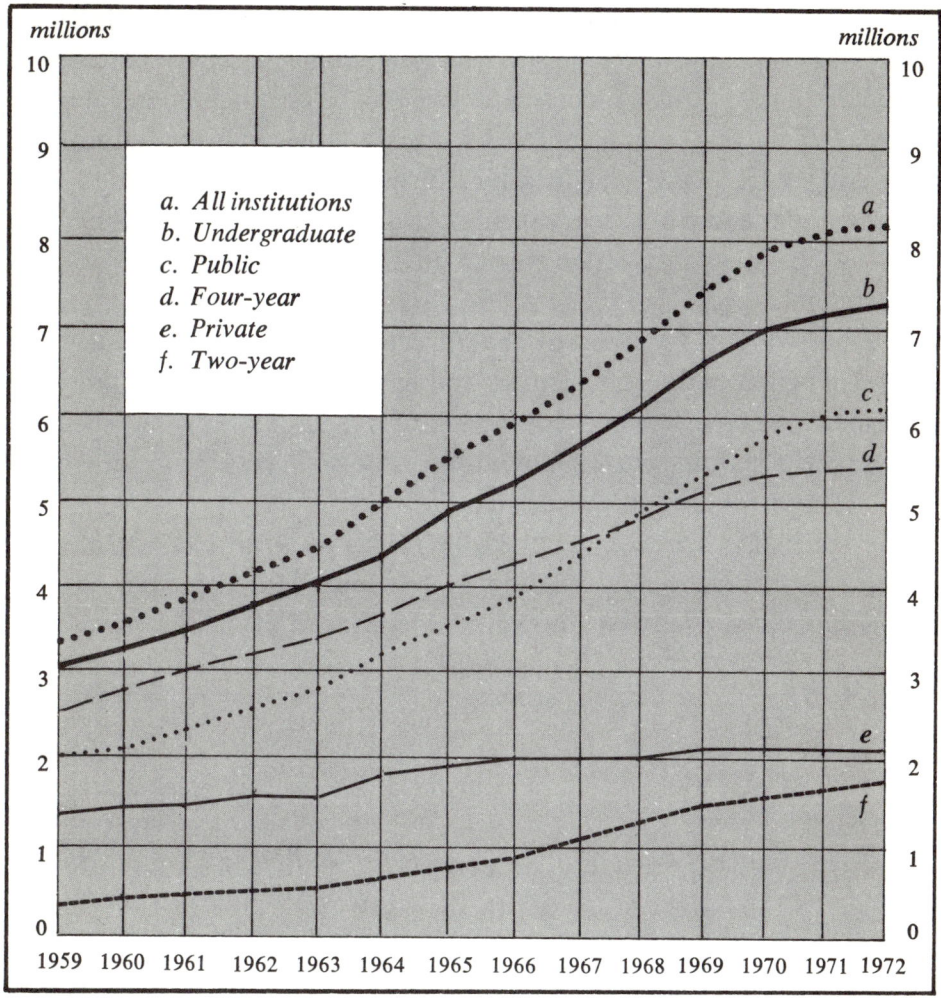

Note: Data for 1972 are based on preliminary estimates.

Sources: U.S. Office of Education, *Projections of Educational Statistics...,* 1970–1972 editions (Washington, D.C.: U.S. Government Printing Office, 1971–1973).

Two major financial issues have emerged from these cost pressures. On the one hand, many private institutions are unable to raise tuition levels high enough to cover rising costs because of the competition from public institutions, many of which provide comparable schooling at lower prices and are often closer to the student's home. On the other hand, public institutions find it difficult or impossible to secure expanded or even constant appropriations from state legislatures, which face increasing demands on public funds for other purposes.

This describes briefly the central problem of colleges and universities today, namely, a serious and widening financial gap as increases in costs continue to outrun increases in revenues. Unless the financial trend is reversed, the nation will confront a decisive crisis in higher education: a lowering of the quality of education, the financial failure of needed institutions, and the loss of access to schooling for thousands of youths.

Colleges and universities often are not well equipped to cope with the economic forces that are now affecting them. This policy statement is an attempt to come to grips with the situation. We propose principles and modes of action in the management and financing of undergraduate education that we believe will encourage the survival of strong and effective institutions providing the high-quality education necessary to satisfy the needs of individuals and the nation.

Our statement is concerned only with *undergraduate* education (postsecondary schooling leading to the baccalaureate degree). We recognize, of course, that undergraduate education cannot always be

---

Figure 2. *The rate of cost increase per student has exceeded the rate of inflation in recent years. In constant 1969–70 dollars, the average cost to colleges per full-time equivalent (FTE) student rose from $1,523 in 1960 to an estimated $2,152 in 1972. This, together with growing enrollment, has resulted in a continued increase in the ratio of higher-education expenditures to GNP (from 1.3 per cent in 1959–60 to about 2.7 per cent in 1971–72), as Figure 2 indicates. These increases in the burden of higher education, which involve a shift of expenditures away from other purposes to meet college costs, are attributable largely to the failure of colleges to increase their productivity. As measured by such quantitative factors as student credit hours, productivity for a long time remained more or less constant in higher education. In a period of rapid inflation its effect upon costs and its demand for a larger share of income are dramatic.*

Figure 2
Expenditures by Institutions of Higher Education, 1959–60 to 1971–72

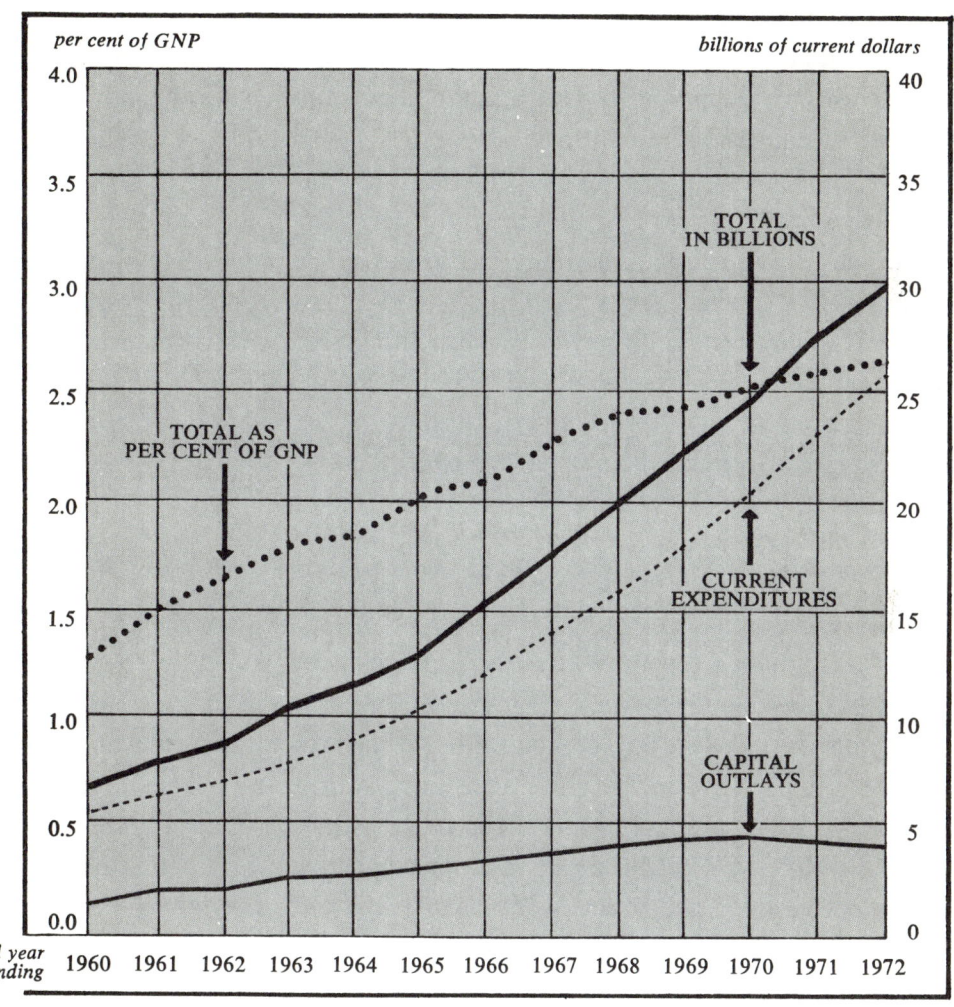

Sources: Expenditures and outlays are estimated in U.S. Office of Education, *Projections of Educational Statistics . . .*, 1970–1972 editions. Percentages of GNP are calculated from U.S. Office of Management and Budget, *The Budget of the United States Government, 1974* (Washington, D.C.: U.S. Government Printing Office, 1973).

separated from graduate and professional education. Many of our recommendations will be applicable to all levels and types of institutions.

In discussing the management of colleges, we are not suggesting that colleges and universities are to be treated as if they were industrial plants or businesses. We fully respect the unique character of education among social and cultural institutions. But we recognize that schools and colleges must raise and expend large sums of money, construct and maintain expensive physical plants, deploy the services of faculty members and a considerable number of personnel, deal with the public and legislatures, and often invest large endowment funds for financial gain. These resources must be managed—and managed effectively—if colleges are to succeed as educational institutions.

The intent of this statement is to bring about greater understanding of these problems and of suggested means of improvement by leaders in business, government, and the professions and among the general public. We especially urge that it be read by college and university trustees and presidents, on whom rests the primary responsibility for action, and by college faculties and student leaders, whose active interest and support in management are essential to major institutional improvements.

A Two-Part Strategy

Although a few institutions are now showing some improvement, many of our colleges and universities continue to be in financial trouble or are on the way to trouble. According to the Association of American Colleges, the number of private accredited four-year colleges and universities running current-fund deficits increased from about one-third of all institutions in 1968 to nearly 60 per cent by 1971.[2] Furthermore, a study of the budget problem confronting forty-one private and public colleges and universities, made by the Carnegie Commission on Higher Education in 1971 and repeated in the spring of 1973, indicated that the situation has not shown any real signs of improvement.[3] Of the eleven

---

2/William W. Jellema, "The Financial Condition of Institutions of Higher Education and the Expenditures That Brought Them to It," Supplementary Paper (New York: Committee for Economic Development, forthcoming).

3/Earl F. Cheit, *The New Depression in Higher Education: Two Years Later* (Berkeley: Carnegie Commission on Higher Education, 1973).

institutions that were "in financial difficulty" in 1971, six were better off two years later, two were in worse positions, and three reported no change. Of the eighteen "headed for financial trouble," half had improved, but the other half had slipped. The twelve institutions "not in financial trouble" also reported mixed results. Only one institution showed an improvement, six were in the same position, and five had slipped.

There have been steep cutbacks in cost among these forty-one institutions, mainly through holding down faculty salaries and cutting maintenance. Some of these costs cannot be deferred indefinitely. Corroborative data also indicate that in order to avert financial deficits many institutions have made significant retrenchments in programs.[4] Such means of cost reduction may help temporarily to close the funding gap, but if colleges are to remain strong, there must be (1) increased income through higher tuition, (2) increased support from government, (3) larger gift income, (4) greater overall efficiency in the use of resources, (5) reduction in programs, or (6) some combination of these.

From our studies we conclude that colleges must take into account two fundamental conditions if they are to develop a realistic financial strategy for the 1970s.

First, because recent predictions of enrollment trends have proved most unreliable, we believe it is wiser, not to base policy on speculation about future trends, but rather to accept slower growth as a premise in planning. Planning should concentrate on consolidation, reorganization, and management improvement during a period of continued slowing of growth. It is always easier to cope with unexpected growth than with unanticipated declines. We do not, however, advise against the establishment of new community colleges where there is a clear need for an expansion of two-year instruction.

Second, we expect that in the decade ahead some additional resources may be obtained from government sources, and we assume that these increases will at least keep pace with increases in student enrollment and the cost of living. This means that we expect government support of higher education on a per student basis to remain more or less constant in real terms. Certainly, we do not anticipate the kind of large increases in governmental funding that occurred during the 1960s.

4/Garven Hudgins and Ione Phillips, *People's Colleges in Trouble* (Washington, D.C.: National Association of State Universities and Land-Grant Colleges, 1971).

Although the future financial health of colleges depends in part on increased revenues, it clearly requires a major dampening of the trend toward disproportionately increasing costs. Holding down costs is largely a problem of management of educational resources. In our view, improved management is the first part of an effective financial strategy for colleges. We therefore devote the earlier chapters of this policy statement to this topic.

If productivity in the colleges does not increase at the same rate as in the economy generally, the amount needed to make up the difference will have to come from sources other than government. The student and his family constitute the only other major source of the funds available to pay for lagging productivity (i.e., cost increases per student in excess of those generated by inflation) and for quality improvement where improvement means increased costs. We believe that total private support through tuition and fees can be increased, assuming that government support is reallocated in ways that will make these increases less burdensome and more equitable. This second part of a financial strategy for colleges is discussed in Chapter 6.

Diversity and Quality

Managing the affairs of a college or university is different in a number of ways from managing a business. Basic, distinctive factors are the collegial or shared-responsibility approach to academic affairs, the tenure of the senior faculty, and the nonquantitative nature of the academic "product." In education there is unusual dependence on voluntary group effort and broad participation in decision making. Many factors in academic affairs resist efficiency and do not lend themselves to typical management techniques. Nevertheless, the welfare of individual institutions and the well-being of higher education generally require that college resources be utilized in a manner that will produce maximum effectiveness in the educational process.

Although we expect that institutions of higher education must face stringent financial circumstances in the decades ahead, we are not willing to conclude that this must result in a lowering of their educational quality. It is a basic position of this policy statement that the quality of postsecondary education must and can move steadily upward through improved use of resources and the careful allocation of funds to high-priority objectives. The answer to slowing enrollments and decreased revenues is better management of educational institutions to provide resources for better education—education that will be recognized as better by students and their parents and by legislators and others who appropriate funds for its support.

There is a growing uncertainty among the American people whether a college education still has the high value once placed upon it. If the leaders of the nation's colleges are to negotiate adequate financial support for the future, their task is not simply the restoration of confidence in particular institutions; even more, it is the cultivation of a new confidence in the basic worth of higher education. In order to achieve this goal, colleges and universities, while preserving whatever is of permanent worth from the past, must be open for experimentation with new forms of education that will fulfill the changing needs of the public as well as the aspirations of individuals.*

We regard educational diversity as essential to the individualism that is basic to the culture and national life. Moreover, diversity in the type and character of colleges and universities—in such matters as educational purposes and goals, instructional programs, types of facilities and students, institutional size and location, bases of funding, and types of organization and control—serves the nation's varied manpower requirements. The nation needs a broad range of educational institutions, extending from technical colleges and community colleges to liberal arts colleges, universities, and advanced technical schools. Quality education—education that achieves goals which serve the interests of individuals and society—is possible in all types of institutions.**

Better Management of Resources

We believe that the best course for every institution to follow is to identify its own distinctive and genuine strengths and then build on those strengths. Its educational programs should exploit its best resources and support goals appropriate to its character. In this way an institution

---
*See Memorandum by MR. THEODORE O. YNTEMA, page 86.
**See Memorandum by MR. WILLIAM M. ROTH, page 86.

can gain in quality and public confidence and contribute, incidentally, to the total diversity of the culture.

Establishing the mission and goals of the institution is the first step toward the effective use of resources. As a next step, every college should develop a strategy that will successfully guide the institution toward those goals. The strategy should be concerned with the type of educational program that should be pursued and the students who should be recruited and admitted. Among other things, it should provide specific reasons why students should attend the institution, faculty should teach in it, and funds should flow to it.

Every institution should seek to develop a strong commitment by the faculty to its goals and strategy complementing their professional commitment to their own disciplines. To achieve this objective, basic principles and guidelines for the administration and management of the institution must be made clear, beginning with goals and including organization, educational policies, planning, and budgets.

The organizational structure of the college or university (i.e., faculty, programs, and departments) should be designed to carry out the strategy effectively. However, there is a challenge in adapting managerial principles derived from other sectors of society to the academic setting. It should be recognized that the realities of the university authority structure place a greater premium on leadership by the president and other administrators than is needed in business or government.

An institution's strategy is basically a matter of long-range planning. There should also be short-term planning that is reflected in annual budgets. In order to make and carry out effective plans, a college needs extensive information such as financial and operating data on all significant phases of operations and costs, including the educational program. Many colleges have made substantial progress in planning and in control of operations and costs. Most of them employ modern machine and computer technologies in gaining and communicating information.

Certain fundamentals of effective management admittedly are difficult to employ in a college or university. There are problems, for instance, in establishing techniques of accountability because of the formidable difficulties encountered in developing measures of performance. But progress is being made and must continue. The important thing is to determine what can and what cannot and should not be done in the effort to improve an institution's effectiveness.

This statement is not designed as a how-to manual on the management of colleges. We simply desire to emphasize the importance of good management if resources are to be employed effectively and efficiently and to urge that every institution make the most of management policies that have proved effective both in education and elsewhere. Experience has already shown that many principles of management employed in other fields can be adapted successfully to institutions of higher learning. Accomplishing this requires strong leadership from the president, resolute support from the trustees, and cooperation from the faculty.

Better management of resources should be made the foundation for increased funding. We believe that the recommendations which we develop in this policy statement, if followed, will do much to stimulate better management and thereby lead to more adequate funding.

Goals and Funding Patterns

We have identified six general purposes of higher education as the basis for specific institutional missions, goals, and objectives. We believe that the funding of institutions should be directed to specific goals which relate to these purposes.

Knowledge and the stimulation of learning. The primary function of a college or university undergraduate program is teaching-learning. It is the generation and dissemination of knowledge and the discipline of the intellect. It entails induction into the uses of reason, the cultivation of critical intelligence, and the stimulation of a continuing desire to learn. The full development of the individual also requires the refinement of the moral and aesthetic sensitivities and the cultivation of a concern for human values.

An educated citizenry. We believe that the strength of democracy in the nation depends to an important degree on an educated citizenry. Elementary and secondary schools provide the basic literacy and communication skills essential to good citizenship.* But the development of public policy, the conduct of public affairs, and the cultivation of the discriminating intelligence essential to civic leadership depend generally on more advanced education.

---

*See Memorandum by MR. ROBERT C. WEAVER, page 86.

Education for the achievement of specific social objectives. The many important goals sought by society allow great leeway for an individual institution in determining the particular area or areas of knowledge and skills on which it can most effectively concentrate. Other institutions will find that their capabilities move them in other directions, and they will attract a different group of scholars and students. No single institution can do all that higher education must accomplish.

Supplying trained men and women. Although we commonly think of professional education as graduate education, the majority of undergraduate degrees granted are in effect professional degrees. Obvious examples are degrees in engineering, education, business, and the fine arts. Thus, even at the undergraduate level, the training of professional workers is an important goal of colleges and universities. A major educational development of recent years is the trend toward the preparation of paraprofessionals, many of whom are trained at the undergraduate level. The human-services occupations are burgeoning, especially in allied health fields and social services. Community colleges, technical colleges, and proprietary schools train many of these paraprofessionals, but traditional four-year colleges are assuming a larger role in their education.

Equality of opportunity. Education beyond high school is often an important factor in determining an individual's chances of achieving economic success and of attaining the life-style to which he or she may aspire. Equality of postsecondary educational opportunity, therefore, is essential to providing each person a fair chance to move into and along the mainstream of socioeconomic life. But individuals from higher socioeconomic backgrounds currently attend colleges and universities at rates that exceed by as much as nine to one those of individuals from the least-advantaged backgrounds. Our recommendations on financing higher education are designed to diminish this disparity.

Economic growth and productivity. The contribution of higher education to economic growth and productivity comes about especially through the education of technical and professional people and managerial leaders and through the creation of new knowledge and the development of its practical uses. Although the creation of knowledge occurs largely in graduate research activities rather than undergraduate education, the two are mutually involved, and it is difficult to separate them completely.

These six basic purposes of higher education are not mutually exclusive; resources expended primarily for one may also support others. Nor will any single technique of funding effectively support all our goals. We recommend, therefore, a pluralistic pattern of funding. Because of the individual benefits, we regard it as appropriate for students and their families to pay as large a part of the cost of their education as they can afford. In the same way, because of the extensive social values of education and society's dedication to the equalization of opportunity, we do not recommend that all or even most students be required to pay the full cost of their schooling through tuition and fees. On the contrary, we advocate in principle government subvention of both institutions and individuals.

Two criteria for establishing satisfactory relationships between goals and funding patterns should be recognized: *appropriateness* and *effectiveness*. A funding pattern is appropriate if it is directed toward agreed-upon goals. It is effective if it produces consequences essential to achieving those goals. Our recommended changes are a matter of targeting funds more accurately for definite goals rather than a movement in totally new directions. This is a system of compromises, but it supports the purposes of higher education, recognizes basic social ideals, and confronts realistically the facts of political power.

SUMMARY OF RECOMMENDATIONS

Following are the major recommendations made by the Research and Policy Committee to improve the management and financing of undergraduate education. These are interspersed with summaries of supporting recommendations.

Goals, objectives, and accountability. Within the general framework of the broad educational purposes just described, each institution should set its own mission, defined in terms of the goals that guide its educational program. These goals must be made operational by the identification of specific objectives to be reached along the way.

We recommend that each college and university establish a policy committee with responsibility to define the long-range goals of the institution and develop a strategy for guiding it in achieving them. Individual

division or departmental policy committees should define the specific instructional objectives that must be reached in the pursuit of the institution's goals.

Goals and objectives change with changing circumstances. Administrative officers and faculties should develop principles and techniques not only for defining and pursuing the institutional goals that are agreed upon but also for periodically reassessing both goals and objectives. Moreover, if goals are to be more than abstract ideals, methods of accountability must be developed that will yield a credible assessment of quality and productivity and will secure for the institution the support of its public.

Management responsibility and authority. Effective college management is a shared responsibility that involves the trustees, the president and administrative staff, the faculty, and in some matters, student representatives. In defining the decision-making process in colleges, we strongly endorse the reserved-powers principle, under which the president assumes all executive powers except those expressly reserved to the governing board or others.

The distribution of managerial responsibility must be matched by an equivalent and explicit distribution of decision-making authority. Those who are held accountable must have the power of action.

The trustees have the ultimate responsibility for institutional decisions, a responsibility they share with the president. We recommend that all executive powers not exercised by or reserved to the trustees or explicitly delegated to others rest with the president. The president, as the chief executive officer, is responsible directly to the trustees. Others to whom responsibility and authority are delegated should be accountable to the president.

By long-established practice, the development of educational policy is a responsibility of the faculty, subject to final approval by the trustees.

We strongly support the principle that faculties should perform a major role in the governance of colleges and universities and in the management of their educational affairs. An institution without strong faculty involvement in governance and management deprives itself of major professional resources that it needs to design and pursue effectively a high-level educational program. Matters in which the faculty should have a predominant voice include admission and retention standards, in-

troduction of programs and courses, requirements for graduation, and recruitment of both faculty and students.

We commend the institutions that have successfully incorporated student representation in their decision-making processes, but we believe that clear limits should be set on this involvement.

Students should have major but not exclusive responsibility for student affairs. They should provide advice for decisions in matters such as course and teacher evaluation, grading practices, curriculum development, student discipline, and selection and retention of certain personnel.

Management and educational policy. While recognizing and preserving the important unique characteristics of educational institutions, the administrative officers of colleges and universities should make the best possible use of management principles and techniques that have proved effective in business and government and are appropriate to the affairs of their institutions.

Because we are convinced that careful planning is essential to the survival of many colleges and universities, we recommend that modern techniques for both long- and short-range planning be utilized by all institutions of higher education.

In higher education, the principal source of possible savings lies in instruction. We urge that administrators and faculties be open to experimentation in this field because we are convinced that there are possibilities here not only for realizing large economies but also for improving the quality of instruction and the excitement of learning.

We recommend that colleges and universities explore the possibilities of new modes of instruction, new types of curricula, new educational timetables, and alternative methods of degree granting in order to provide wider diversity of educational opportunities and the greatest possible effectiveness in the use of resources.

Still other strategies for economy lie in such techniques and programs as cooperative education, consortia developed with other institutions, and institutional amalgamation.

We urge the trustees, administrators, faculties, and students of institutions of every type to consider ways of improving education and at the same time effecting economies through (1) the planned regulation of the growth and size of their institutions and (2) cooperative ventures with other colleges and universities, social agencies, and business and industry.

Academic freedom, job security, and due process. Among major distinctive problems impinging on the management and financing of colleges, none is more critical than the preservation of academic freedom. We firmly advocate policies and practices that will protect responsible intellectual freedom on the campus.

We regard tenure as an important—but not sacred—method of protecting academic freedom and assuring continuity of employment for selected faculty members. But we believe also that flexibility must be built into faculty staffing policies. **We recommend that colleges and universities divide their available faculty positions approximately equally between tenure and contract (nontenure) positions.** Furthermore, colleges and universities should devise methods of assessing periodically each tenured and nontenured faculty member's competence and performance in teaching and research. They should develop programs for the updating and renewal of their faculties.

Finally, we recognize that there is a growing movement toward formal legal action when individuals or groups feel aggrieved by institutional policy. To perpetuate freedom of inquiry, ensure a free and open society on campus, and maintain institutional responsiveness to the individual, we urge the development of carefully written rules, procedures, and guidelines.

We strongly urge that all colleges and universities establish appropriate procedures of due process to guarantee the scrupulous observance of principles of justice and equity in all matters pertaining to faculty, students, and employees.

A strategy for better-targeted and increased financial support. Those who stand in greatest need of financial assistance because of disparities in family income actually now receive a disproportionately small share of governmental aid. We believe that the large task of extending equality of educational opportunity can best be achieved by increased grants and loans made directly to students.

We recommend that federal funding of undergraduate education be primarily through grants and loans to individual students in accordance with their ability to pay. We also recommend that funding patterns of state governments place more emphasis on grants and loans to students according to the same criterion. We further urge that wherever possible the federal government employ its undergraduate financial assistance in a manner which will contribute to more equal educational

opportunity among the states. The financial inequalities between states place this responsibility on the federal government.*

Tuition typically does not pay for the full cost of education. Moreover, there is often an increased cost for educating the economically disadvantaged. We urge that student support in the form of direct student grants be accompanied by grants to the institutions in which those students enroll to cover a part of the additional cost incurred by their enrollment.

If middle- and upper-income families are to finance a greater share of their college costs, as we believe appropriate, the student-loan market must ensure that these families as well as low- and moderate-income families have access to capital. **We recommend an expanded federally operated student-loan system to provide students and their families guaranteed access to supplemental funds.****

A second part of the strategy we propose to increase the financial support received by colleges calls for an increase in tuition charges and fees where they are relatively low, that is, mainly but not exclusively in the public institutions.***

We believe that tuition charges at many colleges and universities are unjustifiably low. We recommend an increase in tuitions and fees, as needed, until they approximate 50 per cent of instructional costs (defined to include a reasonable allowance for replacement of facilities) within the next five years. For two-year community colleges and technical colleges, we recommend that the increase be phased over ten years.****

Government support of both institutions and students is the best means of achieving the various goals of education. Student support serves the goal of equality of opportunity. Such goals as the acquisition of knowledge and the stimulation of learning can best be achieved by institutional grants and appropriations because these goals require direct institutional action in establishing and maintaining instructional programs.

We recommend the continuation of general-purpose grants and appropriations to institutions as the primary form of funding by state and local governments. The amount of these grants and appropriations should be based on undergraduate enrollment and type of undergraduate institu-

---

*See Memorandum by MR. HERMAN L. WEISS, page 86.
**See Memorandum by MR. WILLIAM M. ROTH, page 87.
***See Memorandum by MR. HERMAN L. WEISS, page 87.
****See Memorandum by MR. ROBERT C. WEAVER, page 87.

tion. **They should be available to all types of public or tax-supported institutions.**

Although many private institutions now have student vacancies, some public institutions are overburdened with undergraduate students.

We recommend that state and local governments contract with private colleges and universities to provide undergraduate, professional, and graduate education where public facilities are not adequate. In this way, underutilized private resources will be put to use instead of being duplicated at additional cost.*

In the interest of achieving specific social or technological objectives, it is often advisable for the federal or state governments to fund specific educational programs.

We recommend a system of federal and state categorical grants to both public and private institutions to fund special educational programs designed to meet particular social objectives where those programs cannot be financed from regular budgets or private grants.

As a strategy for increasing the funding of colleges, it is vitally important to encourage more private gift-giving, which has provided an essential margin for educational quality.

We urge that the existing tax incentives for voluntary support of higher education be maintained and, to the extent not incompatible with other objectives, expanded in order to strengthen the base of financial support of all colleges and universities.**

---

*See Memorandum by MR. WILLIAM M. ROTH, page 88.
**See Memorandum by MR. HERMAN L. WEISS, page 88.

Chapter 2
Goals, Objectives, and Accountability

In the coming decade, the financial strength of the nation's colleges and universities will depend in part upon their achieving both effectiveness and efficiency in the use of their resources. An efficient employment of resources has the obvious effect of extending their usefulness; increased efficiency and effectiveness are major factors in winning the kind of confidence of public and patrons that will ensure continued and increased income. We recognize that some aspects of academic life cannot be readily assessed as efficient or inefficient, and we are opposed to the creation of a cult of efficiency in education that would subordinate ends to means. We believe, however, that efficiency must be a concern of all educational institutions if they are to be effective in achieving their ends in the years ahead.

In the recent past, a number of colleges and universities near financial collapse were rescued by hard but wise decisions that had the concurrence of faculty, administration, and trustees. The crucial decisions usually are concerned with educational priorities. Which course of action is essential to the established and accepted mission of the college? What are the scope and limitations of that mission? What programs are expendable because they contribute little or nothing to its fulfillment? To what ends should the institution's faculty resources be dedicated? What criteria should determine the establishment of new courses and programs? Who should make that determination?

These and countless other questions must be continually raised and resolved by cooperative effort. They require a grasp of the basic purposes of education, a clear conception of the mission of the institution, and an effective strategy for achieving the agreed-upon goals that guide the institution's educational program and define its mission.

Defining Goals and Setting Objectives

The broad, basic purposes of education identified in Chapter 1 are determined by the nature of the culture, social institutions, and individual interests. It is within the general framework of these purposes that each college or university must define its own goals. Unless these are clear and conform to the unique characteristics and abilities of the institution, its resources may be dissipated in activities that fail to provide the quality of education of which it is capable. Goals should be few in number and must be conceived and formulated with much care. To be operational, the goals must be supported by specific objectives pertaining to instruction, research, and service; these objectives serve as points along the way of the educational program that must be reached progressively if the institution's goals are to be realized.

Establishing basic goals and specific objectives and committing the institution's resources to them according to carefully planned priorities are the basic management tasks of a college or university. This is the joint responsibility of trustees, administration, and faculty. Students, alumni, and community leaders can give valuable assistance when effective techniques of communication and consultation are utilized.

A statement of educational goals and objectives must relate the institution's educational purposes and activities to the daily tasks of management and finance. Unless goals are concrete and specific and point up the mission of the institution, they may produce little more than confusion. Goals should be consonant with the distinctive character of the institution and its established responsibility to the public and its patrons.

They should reflect a realistic assessment of its actual and potential resources in faculty, facilities, and income.

An all-to-common deficiency of goals statements is indulgence in vague, rhetorical, and even vacuous generalities. An effective educational program cannot be planned and executed if the institution's goals are described simply in terms of such general purposes as "preparing the student for a productive career," "stimulating the intellectual life of the student," or "creating good moral character." These are obviously of basic importance, but they must be taken for granted under the broad purposes of education.

If a college is to develop a distinctive mission, its goals must be described in specific terms, such as "preparing not less than one-fourth of the elementary teachers needed by the state over the next five years"; "qualifying students to enter accredited schools of law, medicine, and public administration"; "providing the basic elements of a scientific and liberal education for those intending to seek the Ph.D."; or "promoting the acquisition of knowledge and training in the basic skills essential to [specified types of] technical vocations."

Like goals, objectives must be concrete and specific if they are to have meaning and practical value. Otherwise, there will be no clear reason and justification for making decisions on such matters as the appointment of faculty, admission of students, development of curricula, assessment of quality of programs, or allocation of financial resources to teaching, research, or community services.

The statement of objectives should take a form such as "all students majoring in business and education will be provided a curriculum that will cultivate their sensitivities to social values," or "every graduate with a baccalaureate degree must have demonstrated [a specified level of] competence in American economic history." This is in contrast with such statements as "the college must have competent faculty members on its social science staff," or "only well-prepared students from secondary schools will be admitted."

Clear and forceful statements of mission, goals, and objectives have several values for effective college operation:

> They enhance public confidence in the institution and unite it with the larger community in a common purpose and effort.
>
> They exhibit the institution's priorities in a manner that encourages confidence and credibility.

They are essential to the evaluation of institutional programs and to the establishment of principles and practices of institutional accountability.

They are necessary as bases for effective management procedures and financial analyses in the assessment of institutional costs.

They provide bases and guidelines for the program allocation of available faculty or financial resources.

They are essential to long- and short-range planning, generally recognized as necessary to good management.

Any task that requires the establishment of firm priorities is difficult; the setting of goals and objectives is no exception. We repeat that because this process is basic to the entire educational enterprise of the institution, it entails close cooperative effort on the part of faculty and administration. Responsible decisions on specific goals are impossible unless alternative courses of action are carefully weighed against each other, with due respect for eventual outcomes, real and potential resources, and possible side effects.

It is in the careful setting of both short- and long-range goals that an institution can preserve the uniqueness of its own character and pursue its particular mission. In doing this, it can not only increase its effectiveness and efficiency but also contribute to the basic diversity of the nation's education. When a college or university attempts to be all things to all segments of society, when it yields to every aggressive pressure, or when it fails to govern its decisions by rational priorities, it is on the dangerous road toward educational failure.

In a world characterized by constant change in values as well as in the most effective ways of achieving them, the educational goals and objectives of even old established schools cannot remain completely static and fixed. Goals must be stable enough to permit effective and efficient management, but the specific educational objectives of an institution must be flexible enough to reflect its sensitivities to the changing conditions of a changing world and to the changing fortunes of its own resources. As each objective is reached, moreover, it must be superseded by a new one. Goals and objectives thus require periodic reassessment.

We urge that administrative officers and faculties of all institutions of higher education develop principles and techniques for effectively defining the educational goals of their institutions and for pursuing and assessing objectives that those goals entail.

Effective Educational Planning

A committee for educational planning is an appropriate device for establishing institutional goals and designing strategies for achieving them. The committee should represent the trustees, administration, and faculty and should have advice from both students and alumni as well as from public leaders in general. Cooperation among these groups requires skillful planning, open lines of communication, and unrestricted access to pertinent educational and financial information. Without these, the necessary community of interest may never materialize.

The vital role played by institutions of higher education in determining the course of society and affecting the rate of social and cultural change places a heavy burden of responsibility on those who define and specify a college's goals and objectives. This is a task of genuine statesmanship that calls for a large reservoir of collective knowledge and wisdom and extensive deliberation by competent advisors and decision makers. An effective planning committee requires the services of experts in educational planning. In most institutions, this work should be centralized in an institutional planning office that provides necessary staff support. The committee, through its director, should be responsible to the president and trustees and should make periodic reports of its work to the faculty.

A college or university should expect each of its operating units (such as divisions, departments, or institutes) to develop both practical objectives and strategies for achieving those objectives within the framework of the institution's mission and basic goals. Such plans must be developed and regularly appraised and updated, and their results must be assessed; otherwise, it is not possible for faculty groups, administrative officers, the president, or the trustees to make responsible decisions affecting the course of the institution.

The effective and efficient operation of colleges and universities is complicated by the large measure of independence commonly enjoyed by academic divisions or departments. Added to this is a considerable degree of independence of faculty members in determining their own courses of instruction. These conditions, which obtain especially in large institutions, are important to the cultivation of academic professionalism and high-quality education. An instructor is commonly appointed on the basis of abilities and interests, and unless a large measure of flexibility and freedom is allowed, the institution will not benefit greatly from his or her creative talents. Moreover, the goals of an institution are determined in part by the specialized talents of its faculty. Both their definition and their achievement depend heavily on individual and departmental initiative and action.*

This problem of individual and departmental self-determination versus institutional purposes and authority presents an educational planning body with some extremely sensitive and complex problems that are at times difficult to resolve. Nevertheless, we believe it is possible to achieve a combination of independence and cooperation that fosters in individuals and departments the spontaneity and creativity essential to educational quality and at the same time serves the general mission of the institution. Here as elsewhere, success depends in part on strong, respected leadership.

We recommend that each college and university establish a policy committee with responsibility to define the long-range goals of the institution and develop a strategy for guiding it in achieving them. Individual division or departmental policy committees should define the specific instructional objectives that must be reached in the pursuit of the institution's goals.

Evaluation and Accountability

If its goals and objectives are to be more than abstract ideals, a college or university must be aware of the direction in which it is moving and the results it is achieving. The institution should be prepared, moreover, to show that funds committed to its support will yield significant social and individual benefits and that the benefits are worth their cost.

Here we are concerned with evaluation and accountability. Although it may involve external agencies, evaluation in educational institutions is commonly an internal process and is concerned primarily with effectiveness, that is, the extent to which goals are actually realized. Accountability, on the other hand, often implies accounting to an external agency or group, possibly simply the community or the institution's patrons, and is concerned with both effectiveness and efficiency. It raises the question of the cost of pursuing and achieving the institution's goals

---

*See Memorandum by MR. HERMAN L. WEISS, page 88.

and objectives and asks whether those costs are justified. Needless to say, those institutions that develop programs of self-evaluation and openly account for their actions and expenditures are least likely to be subjected to accountability demands from external or hostile groups.

Evaluation and accountability are possible where quantitative factors predominate and therefore can be measured. Such situations are commonplace in business and industry. Some measurements are also possible in colleges and universities. The function basic to all American higher education, of course, is formal instruction, the quantitative aspects of which can be reported in a number of complementary terms. These include (1) degrees awarded and the cost per degree, (2) enrollment and the cost per student enrolled, (3) student credit hours and the cost of each credit hour, and (4) student-faculty ratios. These data are essential to the competent evaluation of an institution.

Even with steady advances in analytical techniques and learning theory, however, much that pertains to basic educational achievement cannot be represented in quantitative terms. We assume that in principle this will always be the case. This does not mean that valuable and reliable judgments cannot be made on the qualitative facets of an educational institution and its programs. But it does mean that those judgments require great care, experience, and competence and that they should always be subject to correction.

Accountability as a successful procedure in education requires disclosure of the process and the criteria for assessing the quality and quantity of students served, their academic attainments (including degrees earned), and their subsequent achievements. It also requires opportunities to review assessments and to make periodic examinations of the instruments and methods of evaluation.

College trustees, administrators, and faculties should establish acceptable methods of evaluation and accountability to monitor the quality and productivity of their institutions and secure their credibility with the public.

The evaluation of an educational institution often concentrates too narrowly on institutional resources while neglecting the total impact of the institution both on its students and on the community. That impact, of course, depends not simply on the resources of the institution. It is determined as well by the success with which those resources are marshalled in the pursuit of well-defined goals and objectives.

Interest in accountability is especially focused upon the changes a college is able to effect in its students. A college or university should be judged in terms of the character, the quality, and in some respects, the quantity of the education that it produces as well as by such factors as the quality of its faculty, library, and physical plant or the size of its total budget. The challenge in higher education is to raise students to a superior standard of excellence by the time of their graduation, regardless of their competence when they enter college. With excellence as the central concern, acceptable means should be devised for evaluating achievement. Otherwise, it is nearly impossible to demonstrate that increased expenditures can produce any improvement in the quality of graduates.

However, assessing an institution's impact upon its students is technically difficult. The problem is not so much in documenting the changes that occur in the students' knowledge and behavior while they are attending college. It lies, rather, in determining whether the college experience is in reality the cause of the changes.

Attempts to impose value-added tests as measures of the educational effectiveness of a college, or even of specific courses, encounter nontechnical problems of considerable magnitude. There is, for instance, the inevitable temptation to teach the test rather than to direct the student toward the comprehension of a subject. Perhaps direct inquiries in which students are asked what they think of their college experience or of particular instructors or courses are the most practical and reliable means for measuring institutional quality. Such evaluations by students can also provide faculty and administrative officers with information for assessing trends in student interest and concern. In addition, various longitudinal studies of students may help to evaluate the results of particular college programs and courses of study.

Finally, it is important to point out that the competence of graduates is only one aspect of the productivity of colleges and universities. The assessment of higher education must also be concerned with the results of research and with public service in a variety of forms. An institution should be judged not only by the difference it makes in the lives of its students (the level of their knowledge, their intellectual competence, their creativity, their moral and aesthetic sensitivities, their sense of civic responsibility, their ability to pursue productive careers) but also by the difference it makes in the life of the community it serves or in the life of the nation.

Chapter 3
Management Responsibility and Authority

The distribution of responsibility and power in a college or university is complicated by the fact that such an institution is usually hierarchical in structure but functions on a collegial basis. It is collegial in the sense that faculty members and administrative officers customarily share responsibility in the establishment of general institutional goals and in developing proposals, programs, and policies concerning such academic matters as curricula, student admission and retention, and graduation requirements. But it is hierarchical in that managerial responsibility is centered in the offices of department chairmen, deans, vice-presidents, and president, with ultimate authority residing in the trustees or regents.

This means that levels of responsibility and power must be carefully defined in the policy statements and procedures governing every institution. Otherwise confusion is inevitable, with a resulting loss of both effectiveness and efficiency. Responsibility must be clearly assigned, and those who are held responsible must have the authority to decide and to act.

Responsibility and authority cannot be settled once and for all. New developments in society and in the life and structure of an institution require a continuing reappraisal of the institution's power structure. The current trend toward unionization of college and university faculties and the growing judicialization of campuses are instances of developments that make this reappraisal necessary. (These are discussed in Chapter 5.)

The Trustees and Reserved Powers

Even though college or university trusteeships are sometimes elected positions, they are too commonly regarded as essentially honorary, prestigious appointments for those who have made substantial gifts to the institution, who have gained prominence in business or public life, or who have given valuable political service. This is an unfortunate distortion of the meaning and importance of the trustee's role.

Membership on a college or university governing board is properly a position that makes heavy demands on experience, talent, and decision-making abilities. The trustees have the final overall responsibility for the institution. It is imperative that they be willing and able to invest the necessary time and energy to develop and review periodically the general policies that determine and support its goals and operation and to engage actively in the solution of its basic problems.

The trustees should be concerned with such issues as who the students are or should be, the nature and quality of the faculty, admission and retention policies and procedures, and the substantive nature of the curriculum. Too commonly they are completely bypassed in matters of this kind, and their attention and actions are confined to approving capital improvements and fiscal policy. This is not to suggest that trustees should recruit and select the faculty, initiate promotions, or design the curriculum. Such responsibilities are delegated by them to the administration and faculty; the day-to-day business of the institution is ordinarily not the responsibility of trustees. But trustees should be informed on such matters and should participate in the final determination of policy regarding them.

Most importantly, trustees should ask and insist upon satisfactory answers to fundamental pertinent questions: What is the value of this program? Who wants it? What will it cost, and what is the source of the funds? Who is advocating the expansion of Department X, and why? Have the faculty involved been consulted? Has the value of what has been done been carefully assessed? If not, why not? Does the institution have published procedures on matters of promotion, tenure, faculty review, and so forth?

Whatever powers and responsibilities trustees delegate to administrators and faculties, they themselves are still accountable for ensuring the successful conduct of the institution. They must take the ultimate and decisive actions or be ready to endorse or reject those actions when taken by others. Unless they accept this responsibility, there is danger of deterioration in the quality of administration and management at every level. Moreover, when trustees default in their responsibilities, they invite increased intrusion by external forces such as state legislatures into the internal affairs of public and possibly even private institutions.

Many impressive successes in American higher education have been due to the initiative and decision of trustees who have provided strong institutional leadership. On the other hand, we believe that some institutional failures, especially financial failures, could have been avoided if on crucial occasions the trustees had insisted upon full information disclosure, carefully reviewed goals, changed objectives, re-ordered priorities, canceled programs, or even replaced the president.

One of the fundamental principles to be set forth in the formal code of regulations governing the institution is whether the relationship between the trustees and the president is one of *delegated powers* or *reserved powers*. Under the delegated-powers principle, the president is at liberty to exercise only those duties expressly assigned to him by the terms of his appointment or by subsequent action of the trustees. Under the reserved-powers principle, the president is expected to assume all executive powers except those expressly reserved to the governing board or others.

We strongly endorse the reserved-powers principle, which we believe is conducive to strength in presidential leadership. Unfortunately, this fundamental issue of responsibility and power is seldom resolved satisfactorily in colleges and universities. Unless it is resolved through a clear delineation of the powers belonging to the trustees and to the president, effective leadership is endangered. A reserved-powers arrangement requires the president to function as a more broadly responsible manager. We believe this leads to more effective administration and management.

The trustees, of course, have the important power of appointing and removing the president. Moreover, they have the power of final approval for all major institutional decisions. However, as we have already indicated, the power of trustees should not be regarded simply as power of approval, which suggests a rubber-stamp function. Their task in the institution should not be passive; rather, it should be constructive and positive in a manner that will not interfere with the responsibilities and prerogatives of administrators and faculty.

We recognize, of course, that different approaches to their tasks are appropriate for the trustees of different kinds of institutions. We have no desire to prescribe one format for their activities. The trustees of a small private college in a small community may properly play a substantially different role from that of the trustees of a large tax-supported urban university.

State Systems

In state systems where there are state boards of control or coordinating bodies in addition to individual institutional boards, or even where no separate institutional boards exist, there are additional problems of responsibility and power. Confusion and conflict can develop unless the enabling legislation and operating policies are clear and the delegations of duties and authority are definite and explicit. Indeed, many of the most difficult administrative and management problems today have resulted from the creation of state boards.

Boards that control several institutions must guard against becoming separated or even alienated from them. It is unfortunate when the actual governing board is regarded by the administration or faculty as an outside agency. When this occurs, the board may become more a block than a support to the institution's development. A coordinating council or state board can sap both the strength and the will of an institution if it fails to perform a fundamentally supportive role and becomes instead an obstacle to change and progress through its power over such matters as new programs. There is also the danger that in guarding against unwise duplication of programs and services among the institutions they control, state boards will inadvertently create extensive and expensive staffs that are unnecessary in view of the resources already resident in those institutions.

On the other hand, state councils and boards can become sources of major strength to an institution. We believe that the complexity of the higher-educational enterprise and the high costs of education justify the existence of these bodies. Without them, individual institutions have often engaged in unnecessary duplication of effort and expenditure and unwise competition that have been wasteful and inefficient. The problem is to make sure that the benefits of effective leadership and cooperation are realized through systems of coordination without losing the benefits of diversity among the constituent institutions and the initiative and vitality that reside in their faculties and administrative staffs.

We recognize the great worth to the society of diversity among educational institutions, and we believe that this diversity should be cultivated and protected. **We urge that both external agencies and system governing boards not raise obstacles to diversity among institutions of higher education but rather establish policies and practices that will preserve and cultivate diversity.***

Reasonable autonomy of colleges and universities consistent with public accountability is essential to maintaining institutional diversity and the quality of higher education. Although we recognize that no institution can or should have absolute independence, especially when it is a part of a higher-education system, we believe that care should be taken to avoid the erosion of autonomy by outside forces. **We strongly urge that every institution, in cooperation with the governmental and other agencies with which it is associated, identify the proper limits of its autonomy.**

The President

In general, the position of president of a college or university has been severely weakened in recent years. If the nation's institutions of higher education are to have the quality of management that they will need in the future, the president must be strengthened by a clear commitment of the trustees to support his use of all executive powers except those that have been specifically assigned to others or expressly retained by the governing board. The president cannot provide genuine leadership if his actual authority is only marginal.

---

*See Memorandum by MR. JOSEPH L. BLOCK, page 88.

A college or university is legally accountable to its governing board. Its president must make sure that the trustees understand and support the institution. In pursuit of this end, the president must engage the trustees in periodic reviews of institutional goals and priorities. He must make regular reports that will enable them to arrive at informed judgments about the direction of the institution's programs and the wisdom of its policies.

We realize that the president's role is inevitably complicated not only by the great variety of tasks he must pursue as educator, administrator, and manager but also by the wide dispersion of decision-making activities and powers characteristic of an educational institution. It is largely because of the dispersion of authority and the ambiguous nature of his position that a president may find it extremely difficult to achieve satisfactory results in defining his institution's goals effectively and directing its energies toward their realization. He must function both as chief executive of a large organization and as a colleague of the faculty.

The president's responsibility for the day-to-day management of the institution requires that he have the power, after appropriate consultation, to select the individuals who are to serve as members of his management team and to remove them when necessary. He must have the power to delegate specific duties to members of his administration, prepare the budget for final consideration by the trustees, represent the institution in its contacts with other organizations and agencies, and deal directly or through his designated representatives with faculty, staff members, and students on matters of institutional policy and operation.

Without the goodwill or at least the acceptance by a large number of external constituencies, a college or university can rarely prosper—and may not even survive. The president, therefore, cannot escape devoting much of his own and his administrative staff's time to efforts to cultivate relations that will serve both the immediate and the long-term interests of the institution. The president and trustees can serve as effective representatives to such agencies as legislative bodies, alumni groups, business associations, and labor organizations. Without surrendering any of the institution's initiative or responsibility for internal decisions, the president should enlist those agencies in active support of its goals.

A president's decisions and actions may be affected or determined by a large number of external organizations such as legislatures, accrediting agencies, unions, professional associations, state civil service systems, central purchasing agencies, or state finance departments, not to mention the numerous agencies of the federal government that fund projects and programs on college and university campuses. In dealing with his multiple constituencies and carrying out his many and sometimes conflicting roles, the president cannot rely simply on the formal authority that is based on the sanctions and powers inherent in his office and specified in the trustees' regulations. He must develop an essentially functional authority based on competence, integrity, trust, skill in leadership, and personal persuasiveness. He must lead through his ability to elicit from his colleagues their best efforts and their full commitment to building an institution of high quality.

The president's effectiveness depends in part, of course, on the quality of the administrative staff and his relations with that staff. His leadership is in large part exercised through the central administrative staff, the deans, and the department chairmen. They must all have a genuine capacity for educational leadership combined with managerial ability. It is important, of course, for the president to include on his central staff people with special competence in modern management processes and legal procedures.

The distribution of managerial responsibility must be matched by an equivalent and explicit distribution of decision-making authority. Those who are held accountable must have the power of action.

The trustees have the ultimate responsibility for institutional decisions, a responsibility they share with the president. We recommend that all executive powers not exercised by or reserved to the trustees or explicitly delegated to others rest with the president. The president, as the chief executive officer, is responsible directly to the trustees. Others to whom responsibility and authority are delegated should be accountable to the president.

The Faculty

Unfortunately, there seems to be a growing attitude among American college and university faculties that the administration is a separate, if not alien, segment of the institution. Although we recognize that certain tensions inevitably develop between faculty and administration, we believe that education will be best served in the future if the cooperative relationships traditional in the nation's colleges and universities are deliberately cultivated and encouraged.

Many colleges and universities have a long tradition of faculty participation in determining basic managerial policies, decisions, and actions. Participation in the management of their institutions arises largely from the responsibilities that faculties commonly have for the determination of educational policy. It is impossible to function effectively in educational matters without becoming involved either directly or indirectly in management.

Where the trustees have delegated the formulation of educational policy to the faculty, the faculty commonly proposes admission and retention standards, initiates new programs and new courses, revises or deletes old courses, and determines requirements for graduation. In addition, faculty members in most colleges and universities participate by means of recommendation in the vital functions of recruitment, retention, promotion, and tenure of academic personnel, even though the official action in tenured appointments and promotions is actually taken by the trustees. In our opinion, it is essential to good administration, as well as to the best professional educational policy, that faculties perform managerial functions such as these, which are related both to their professional competencies and to their basic tasks as teachers and scholars.

Clearly, the quality of the faculty's relationships with the administration and trustees is of central importance to the health of the institution. The participation of faculty in certain areas of management must mean, among other things, access to the information needed for informed decisions and provisions for effective communication between faculty and administration. Unless the appropriate faculty members have certain kinds of financial information, for instance, they cannot make responsible decisions on expanding or deleting educational programs.

We strongly support the principle that faculties should perform a major role in the governance of colleges and universities and in the management of their educational affairs. An institution without strong faculty involvement in governance and management deprives itself of major professional resources that it needs to design and pursue effectively a high-level educational program. Matters in which the faculty should have a predominant voice include admission and retention standards, introduction of programs and courses, requirements for graduation, and recruitment of both faculty and students.

Although the administrative structure of an institution may be expected to vary in accordance with its type and, especially, its size, it is obvious that the faculty can function responsibly and effectively only if there are generally accepted provisions for the formation, expression, and communication of opinions and plans, such as various kinds of representative committees, commissions, and legislative bodies. Our concern is simply to ensure that for the countless activities requiring faculty opinion and action (from departmental decisions to major institutional policies), the methods of faculty participation and representation are adequate.

For typical institutions, we strongly favor representative bodies such as faculty or university senates to legislate on academic matters affecting the entire institution. We favor democratic action also at the college and department levels. Faculty representation on commissions or committees concerned with such matters as appointments, promotions, tenure, academic freedom, long-range planning, discipline, and college and university goals is essential. Most institutions will now find an executive committee composed largely of elected faculty members to be essential to cooperative action by the administration and faculty.

The Students

We believe that effectiveness in college and university management in the future depends in considerable part on the role of students in making decisions on matters intimately affecting them. It is important to the vitality of any educational institution that it be responsive to student needs, interests, and problems. This means, of course, that students must be prepared to accept a large measure of responsibility.

Today's students are demonstrating their capacity to assume important institutional responsibilities beyond their primary function as learners. They are gaining a larger role in determining the conditions of their membership in the academic community. They are being included both formally and informally in decision-making councils. They are providing input for decisions relating to course and teacher evaluation, grading practices, curricular innovations, departmental and college planning, program development, student discipline, and even the selection of presidents and faculties. In student government and in managing substantial funds in the form of student fees, they are taking new initiative and responsibility.

We commend the many colleges and universities that have successfully incorporated student representation in their decision-making processes. We believe that clear limits should be set on student power; the primary role of the student is that of learner, not manager. But we believe that in matters intimately affecting students, their participation is indispensable.

Acting individually, students exercise an important influence upon the management and financing of colleges in deciding which schools they will attend, as well as in selecting subjects, specific courses, and teachers. As students generally become more independent, and as higher education becomes more susceptible to students' freedom of choice, institutions can be expected to give increasing attention to the kinds of academic programs that students themselves appear to want and to be willing to pay for.

Students should have major but not exclusive responsibility for student affairs. They should provide advice for decisions in matters such as course and teacher evaluation, grading practices, curriculum development, student discipline, and selection and retention of certain personnel. Any college or university that fails to capitalize on the advice and counsel of its students in academic matters is failing to exploit a most valuable asset.

Chapter 4
Management
and Educational Policy

The combined pressures of rising costs and restricted support impose upon colleges and universities the necessity for utmost care in setting priorities and deploying resources. Over the coming decade the possibility of adequately financing higher education will depend to a great extent upon improved management of resources. At the same time that administration and faculty are developing better ways to realize greater returns from their expenditures, they should also be able to make significant improvements in the total educational enterprise. We believe that more effective management of resources can improve educational quality.

Administrative officers of colleges and universities, while keeping in mind the implications for management of the unique characteristics of educational institutions, should become thoroughly familiar with the management principles and techniques that have proved effective in business and government.

We recommend that college and university administrators adopt, when appropriate, the principles and techniques af management that have resulted in increased effectiveness and productivity in other academic institutions and in business and government.

In the adoption of such principles and techniques, it is essential to keep in mind the labor-intensive nature of much of the educational enterprise and to remember that colleges are not comparable to factories or department stores. It should never be forgotten that they exist for educational, not business, purposes. A college or university should be managed as an integrated organization in which the plans and programs of the various operating units are governed by institutional goals, objectives, and priorities. As we have noted, there must be a clear definition of the location of various kinds of decision-making authority, and administrative officers should give particular attention to problems of maintaining effective two-way transmission of information between central academic and business offices and operating units such as colleges, departments, and institutes.

Management Methods and Personnel

Typically, institutions of higher learning have been understaffed in their central management structure. Much of the decision-making authority in colleges and universities is, of course, diffused among the faculty. As we have indicated, we believe that faculty involvement in the determination and implementation of academic policies is an important source of institutional strength. The increasing complexity of institutional management requires that many colleges both enlarge and upgrade their central staffs with professionally competent administrators in order to achieve more efficient use of institutional resources. Those colleges and universities fortunate enough to have competent financial or business managers trained and experienced in the techniques of management should involve them directly in the decision-making process so that their knowledge and experience can influence commitments involving financial resources. Needless to say, the development of congenial working relationships between those having academic and business functions is fundamental to good college and university management.

Individuals in both faculty and staff positions who exhibit ability for leadership should be given opportunities to gain management experience within the institution. Those who demonstrate a capacity for growth and continuing interest in administration should be encouraged to develop a wide range of management skills in preparation for new assignments entailing greater responsibility. They should learn how to make informed decisions, how to live with responsibility, how to set priorities, and how to exercise authority.

In recruiting administrative officers, colleges and universities would be well advised wherever possible to seek candidates who have been successful in similar positions at other institutions. The invigorating cross-fertilization of ideas and perspectives that benefits business corporations when well-qualified executives make intercompany moves can be equally advantageous to institutions of higher education.

As college and university executives endeavor to increase the efficiency of their management procedures, and as they search for more effective solutions to the problems facing higher education in times of financial stress and uncertainty, they may find it advantageous to engage the advisory services of qualified management and financial consultants. Moreover, college presidents should find the business and financial experience of many of their trustees to be valuable sources of advice and guidance in dealing with management problems.

We recommend that colleges and universities recruit and develop personnel who are sensitive to the unique nature and needs of academic institutions and are capable of employing modern management methods.

With the help of their business officers, the executives of a college must at all times be able to ascertain the costs of both academic and nonacademic programs. Accounting procedures must be organized to accept and interpret a wide range of transactions without delay. Even though it is not always easy to do so, academic and business officers should endeavor to pinpoint with reasonable accuracy the value of financial expenditures in terms of expected benefits, academic or nonacademic. It is important that academic administrators and faculty representatives, not business officers, be responsible for decisions on matters of educational policy.

Effective management of internal business functions has become a necessity for all colleges expecting to remain solvent in the face of steadily rising costs. Even colleges fortunate enough to have endowment funds must make certain that those funds are administered by individuals of high integrity and considerable skill and experience. College investment officers should have expert training for this critically important task. They should function with the advice of professionally competent investment counsel and report to competent investment committees.

Investment decisions must be made within the bounds of clearly defined objectives established by the trustees. Although they must respect the values represented by the institution, the investment policies and practices of a college should be fashioned after the policies and practices of successful financial institutions.

Planning and Budgeting

The need for intelligent and effective short- and long-term planning in higher education is more urgent today than ever before. Only through careful planning can colleges and universities expect to be reasonably successful in responding to the financial, social, and political crises of the 1970s and 1980s.

During the 1950s, Beardsley Ruml argued that long-range planning and good management can help colleges achieve more effective utilization of personnel, space, and financial resources. Ruml advocated budgetary control as an instrument for planning because a budget converts everything (including educational programs and objectives) into dollars; this makes it possible to set priorities and maintain control over resources. A budget must balance over a period of time, and someone must know where the money is coming from as well as where it is going.

Many people believe colleges and universities to be wasteful. They see buildings that are not fully utilized; they learn of faculty members who seem to spend very little time teaching. It is our opinion that some of these impressions of waste and inefficiency are justified.* We mention this here because we believe that part of this inefficiency is due to poor planning or no planning at all. In the opinion of some, higher education is facing such momentous changes that planning for the future is impractical. Actually, this very uncertainty heightens the need for both short-term budgeting and long-range planning as devices that enable college executives and trustees to deal with rapid change and sometimes unforeseen events.

Budgets built on the basis of intelligent planning will reflect and support institutional objectives and priorities. Budgets designed to accomplish specific objectives, as opposed to simple line-item budgets, provide college presidents and trustees with a practical method for judg-

---

*See Memorandum by MR. JOHN R. COLEMAN, page 89.

ing the efficiency of the various budget and cost centers in their institutions. Only by planning effectively can colleges retain an appropriate measure of control over their destinies and perpetuate desirable diversity in higher education. It is clear that unless colleges and universities make their own plans, others will impose objectives upon them. Moreover, unless the planning process involves the participation of both faculty and business officers, educational considerations or the material resources necessary to achieve educational ends may be neglected.

Because we are convinced that careful planning is essential to the survival of many colleges and universities, we recommend that modern techniques for both long- and short-range planning be utilized by all institutions of higher education.

Management and the Improvement of Teaching

In higher education, the principal source of possible savings is in instruction. Theoretically at least, increased faculty teaching loads in the form of larger class-size averages would result in significant reductions in the cost of instruction. This is not to argue for more large lecture courses, but rather for fewer unnecessarily small classes.

A major constraint on any such proposal is faculty resistance to the introduction of modern instructional technology. Nevertheless, instructional technology may eventually bring about more productive uses of teacher and student time. It may also provide an effective way for bridging the gap between the classroom and the outside world and for providing access, even in remote rural colleges, to the best teaching and the richest opportunities for learning that are available at the nation's most prestigious colleges and universities.

We urge that administrators and faculties be open to experimentation in this field because we are convinced that there are possibilities here not only for eventually realizing economies but also for improving the quality of instruction and the excitement of learning. Every institution would be well advised to keep instructional experimentation high on its list of priorities.

Improved quality in teaching and learning should be a direct result of strengthened management of the educational process. Here the delegation of management responsibilities to college executives and to the faculty must be coordinated to ensure availability of resources needed to implement specific educational objectives. The following objectives are essential to improving the quality of college instruction:

> Developing more effective and reliable methods for assessing teaching performance by both students and colleagues

> Employing modern instructional techniques and instruments where they can effectively augment the teaching-learning process

> Establishing effective faculty career-development programs through appropriate combinations of in-service seminars, peer evaluations, directed readings, opportunities for innovation, visiting appointments, and paid leaves to gain new knowledge and professional insight

> Modifying the prevailing faculty reward system to ensure more generous recognition for excellence in teaching as well as research

> Strengthening the preparation of prospective college teachers in graduate schools by introducing them to current theories of learning and motivation, by providing them with well-supervised teaching-intern experiences, and by exposing them to superior college teachers.

> Identifying undergraduate students who show ability and encouraging them to prepare for careers as college teachers

We believe colleges should concentrate on developing techniques for evaluating teaching excellence that will enable them to provide special compensation for teachers who successfully challenge, inspire, and lead their students in the quest for knowledge and wisdom and who motivate the students to develop their creative talents. The continuing development of faculty personnel is an objective that colleges can neglect only at the cost of diminished educational quality and productivity.

We recommend that all colleges and universities fashion programs for the continuous professional development of the faculty and that they insist upon continuing achievement in teaching, research, and other activities consonant with institutional goals.

Nontraditional Education

Although it is essential to continue support for those aspects of education that have proved their worth through the years, important changes already appearing in the character of American postsecondary education are certain to have far-reaching consequences for the future of colleges and universities, with resulting challenges for college management. The 1970s are characterized by a critical reassessment of the structure of postsecondary education in terms of the needs of students whose backgrounds and interests differ from the traditional college student population.

There is now increasing interest in a variety of alternative, experimental, and unconventional approaches to postsecondary education. In addition to both professional and public opinion favoring nontraditional arrangements, a restructuring of governmental priorities in financing education may provide added incentives to move postsecondary education in new directions. A major by-product of these developments is the opening of educational opportunities for many people who heretofore have been unable to obtain a higher education. Following are several types of nontraditional education that should receive the attention of college executives and faculty members.

External study under existing curricula leading to traditional degrees. Such arrangements include weekend and evening colleges, combinations of correspondence and on-campus experience, regional learning centers, and broadcast television courses. The British Open University is an excellent example that deserves the closest study.

New time dimensions for learning. This is illustrated by programs for admitting students to college at the end of their junior year of high school, permitting students to carry heavier-than-usual course loads, experimenting with three-year degree programs, and awarding credit on the basis of student competence without course enrollment.*

Certification without instruction. This is the recognition of competence by formally granting credentials or academic degrees for the knowledge and skill that people acquire outside the classroom.

The success with which colleges and universities blend traditional and nontraditional approaches in postsecondary education will determine in part their capacity to respond effectively to the needs of the wide range of students whom they must serve in the years ahead.

We recommend that colleges and universities explore the possibilities of new modes of instruction, new types of curricula, new educational timetables, and alternative methods of degree granting in order to

---

*See Memorandum by MR. JOHN R. COLEMAN, page 89.

provide wider diversity of educational opportunities and the greatest possible effectiveness in the use of resources.

Strategies for Economy

The experience of some institutions suggests that there are various strategies through which colleges and universities may realize important economies while at the same time improving the quality of education that they provide. We urge that the following strategies be examined and considered carefully by the trustees, presidents, and faculties of colleges and universities that may be facing financial difficulties. It is of prime importance, of course, that they not betray their institution's mission—although for good reason they may elect to revise it—and that they not engage in efforts at economy which endanger educational quality.

Optimum institutional size. The size of a college or university, measured by the number of students enrolled, appears to have a direct relationship to institutional costs. According to the economies-of-scale principle, it may be assumed that if a college increases its enrollment, its additional income from student tuition will exceed the additional expenditures it must make to accommodate a larger number of students. However, as colleges achieve substantial increases in student enrollment, they typically aspire to new and more expensive programs, each with special requirements for space and budget and with ambitions to recruit more faculty to teach smaller and fewer classes.

Another consideration that tends to offset economies achieved by scale is the sometimes negative effect of large campuses on the students themselves and on the methods of instruction. As campus enrollment increases, opportunities for participation in important extracurricular activities become available to relatively few students, and larger classes (especially at the freshman and sophomore levels) tend to become lecturing sessions in which students find it easy to lapse into relatively passive attitudes toward learning.

If all institutions of higher education were aiming at the same goals, it would appear feasible to construct a precise table of recommended enrollments related to economies of scale. But since college and university objectives vary, enrollments and costs per student also vary. The optimum size for an educational institution is closely related to its unique character and circumstances, its goals and objectives, and the special expectations of the students it serves. Enrollment ranges should be set carefully in the interest of the greatest efficiencies possible in keeping with an institution's purposes and within the limits of its actual resources.

Cooperative education. Cooperative education is a strategy that incorporates off-campus work as an integral part of the student's educational program. Like other examples of off-campus education, such as independent study and travel abroad, cooperative education is responsive to student needs for individualized and personally relevant education. In addition, most programs of cooperative education offer students some relief from the high costs of education by providing work assignments in the form of paid employment. Typically, students in cooperative-education programs are on campus for all of their freshman year and then alternate between full-time campus study and full-time off-campus work.*

As a consequence of their participation in cooperative education, students develop competencies and insights that assist them in making informed decisions about their future careers. They develop greater confidence in their ability to make independent judgments, find greater meaning in their studies, and gain valuable experience in human relations. Cooperative education has been especially valuable to people from low-income groups because it has made college feasible; likewise, it has proved to be an excellent way to open new career possibilities to people from minority groups and to women. This has been a major reason why many predominantly black colleges have implemented cooperative-education programs.

In addition to its value as a strategy for making education more relevant to the student's nonschool experience, cooperative education has been regarded as a means of conserving an institution's resources and, hence, a way to keep operating costs down. The alternating pattern typically followed by cooperative-education programs will accommodate an increased number of students without additions to the physical plant and with only a modest increase in faculty and support staff. There are two necessary conditions, however, if these savings are to be realized. First, the institution as a whole must follow the cooperative plan. Second, the student enrollment must be increasing. If there are no additional stu-

---

*See Memorandum by MR. HERMAN L. WEISS, page 90.

dents to keep the on-campus population at capacity, instructional costs will rise. If these two conditions are met, it is entirely possible that within a period of five years an institution could move from a deficit to a surplus operation.

Consortia. A college or university consortium is a formal arrangement through which two or more institutions voluntarily agree to cooperate in establishing or futhering programs from which each participating institution expects to obtain some special advantage. Educational consortia are intended to combine the individual strengths of member institutions for the mutual benefit of all.

Consortia can help cooperating colleges and universities retain their distinctive individual characteristics, thus preserving the diversity that is such an important property of American higher education. Consortia can include both public and private institutions. They can help cooperating colleges and universities to be more flexible, imaginative, creative, and experimental; they can cut across state and political boundaries without the necessity of formal governmental action; they can enable institutions to acquire some of the advantages of largeness without the accompanying disadvantages; and they can cultivate a healthy climate for grass-roots decision making and creative faculty participation in institutional governance.

Economies are possible if the participating institutions plan carefully, but this is not the only justification for organizing a consortium. Areas in which a consortium can achieve economies for its members include recruitment of students; services of staff; building use and insurance; joint use of laboratories, observatories, and computer services; printing services and publications; lecture, concert, and museum bookings; health services; operation of museums, athletic facilities, and libraries; joint faculty appointments and faculty exchanges in specialized fields; reciprocal enrollment privileges in specified disciplines; and joint purchasing and accounting procedures.

Institutional amalgamation. Another, although less frequent, strategy for economy is the consolidation of two or more institutions. Of course, not all amalgamations are reactions to financial crises; many are efforts to overcome unnecessary duplication or to improve program quality at the lowest possible cost.

Amalgamation may be particularly advantageous to single-purpose institutions that find themselves obliged to extend their programs in order to satisfy the directives of regulatory agencies or to meet the demands of the marketplace. Under some circumstances amalgamation can be traumatic for the institutions and the individuals directly involved. Innumerable adjustments are required in policies and procedures, in salaries and fringe benefits, in governance and goals. But the financial position of the amalgamated institution should eventually be more favorable than that of its component parts, and it should therefore be more capable of providing quality education.

We urge the trustees, administrators, faculties, and students of institutions of every type to consider ways of improving education and at the same time effecting economies through (1) the planned regulation of the growth and size of their institutions and (2) cooperative ventures with other colleges and universities, social agencies, and business and industry.

Chapter 5
Academic Freedom, Job Security, and Due Process

As we have already recognized, colleges and universities differ from business and industrial organizations in many significant ways. Two of the most important distinguishing characteristics of higher education are a concern for the preservation of academic freedom and the principle and practice of faculty tenure. Both deserve consideration here because they are important in the management of institutions of higher education.

Academic freedom, which is essentially intellectual freedom, is a bulwark in the quest for truth upon which a free society depends. It is the principle that individuals, both faculty and students, should not be inhibited or restrained by external forces or threat of censure in the search for knowledge and the presentation of information and ideas, whether in the classroom, in publications, or through other means of communication.

We believe that responsible academic freedom, which ensures an open forum for ideas, is essential to the vitality of the educational processes through which students are challenged to develop their capabilities for independent thought and the critical evaluation of alternative actions.

Because it is essential to the achievement of a genuinely free society, we urge that all institutions of higher education adopt policies and practices that will establish and protect responsible intellectual freedom on their campuses. We recognize that our most cherished freedoms are grounded in the intellectual life and that constant vigilance is the price of their survival.

Faculty Tenure

Faculty tenure is generally regarded as a necessary means for guaranteeing academic freedom and ensuring fair and equitable treatment of faculty personnel. Nevertheless, tenure is now being severely scrutinized by citizens, legislators, and trustees, some of whom see it as a shield for incompetence or irresponsibility. We believe that as other safeguards of academic freedom become more firmly established in public attitudes, institutional procedures, and legal decisions, faculty tenure may be seen as somewhat less than absolutely essential to either the protection of freedom or the guarantee of fair treatment for faculty members.*

The principle of tenure is entirely defensible. If a tenure system is carefully administered and rigorous standards of selection are maintained so that only highly qualified faculty members achieve tenure, great institutional strength and vitality can result. On the other hand, a poorly managed or seemingly automatic system of tenure can burden an institution with long-term commitments to faculty members who possess only modest abilities and limited interest in professional self-improvement.

During the twenty-five years following World War II, while higher education in the United States was experiencing a remarkable period of growth and expansion, the competition among colleges and universities for well-qualified members led many institutions to grant tenure to relatively young faculty members, many of whom were still serving at the assistant professor level. Consequently, in today's comparatively no-growth period there is some risk that institutions may lose the flexibility they need to respond through faculty appointments to changing educational priorities and to maintain a dynamic balance of experienced and developing faculty talent.

---

*See Memorandum by MR. ELLERY SEDGWICK, JR., page 90.

One possibility for building future flexibility into faculty staffing policies would be a division of available faculty positions into tenure and nontenure. Such a division is already an established and accepted practice at some colleges and universities. Persons appointed to nontenure positions may serve under one-, two-, or three-year contracts and be eligible for reappointment to their nontenure positions or to vacant tenure positions for which they are qualified. In any event, appointments to tenure positions should be reserved for individuals who have demonstrated to both students and colleagues their superior ability as teachers and scholars and their professional commitment to excellence in the pursuit of knowledge and the cultivation of reason. Moreover, these appointments should clearly support the accepted objectives and long-range goals of the institution.

We recommend that colleges and universities divide their available faculty positions approximately equally between tenure and contract (nontenure) positions.*

Tenure should be awarded only as a deliberate institutional decision in which student representatives and nontenured faculty members, as well as tenured faculty members and administrative officers, are involved. Final action in granting tenure should be reserved to the trustees.

If the principle of faculty tenure is to withstand the current wave of criticism, many institutions must find new ways to raise the general level of faculty commitment to self-improvement and professional responsibility. **It is essential that colleges and universities devise methods of assessing periodically each tenured and nontenured faculty member's competence and performance in teaching and research.** These evaluations should be made mainly, but not exclusively, by the individual's faculty colleagues. They are best qualified for such judgments. Ineffective faculty members should at least be directed into appropriate programs of career development to upgrade their teaching abilities and to ensure that they will not become incompetent as teachers or obsolescent in their scholarly disciplines.

The current controversy over tenure is widespread and is not likely to subside in the near future. The choice between traditional faculty tenure and some alternative can best be made in the light of the history, accomplishments, and objectives of each institution. Whatever

---

*See Memorandum by MR. JOHN R. COLEMAN, page 90.

course is taken, we repeat that it should be designed to perpetuate and nourish freedom of inquiry as one of the essential foundations of a free and open society.

Faculty Collective Bargaining

Faculty unions and collective bargaining are now established facts at a large number of institutions, and unionizing activity is gaining ground at many others. However, this is not to say that all faculties will be unionized or that unionization is inevitable in any particular case. On the contrary, it seems quite unlikely that faculty unionization will become universal in American higher education at an early date. Without taking a position either for or against faculty collective bargaining, our concern is that college and university trustees, executives, and faculty members fully examine the implications of unionization for their respective institutions and prepare themselves to face the matter intelligently.

Faculty collective bargaining in colleges and universities has typically resulted in increased salaries and fringe benefits. Salary increases generally have been commensurate with those gained by state civil service employees. There has been a trend toward parity between teaching and nonteaching professionals and toward raising the salaries of community-college and state-college faculties to the level of university faculties at comparable ranks. In private institutions, across-the-board increases are common outcomes of collective bargaining. Unions commonly bargain for formal salary schedules and request extensive access to detailed institutional financial data.

Collective bargaining generates the necessity for an enlarged institutional bureaucracy. Highly qualified personnel directors and special legal counsel, together with their supporting staffs, are often necessary. However, the addition of highly competent personnel officers and legal advisors may result in important improvements in the management of some institutions.

Unions are usually expected to attempt to influence institutional management in such matters as budgeting, course scheduling, work loads, and the assignment of personnel. Some observers expect a loss of educational leadership on the part of the president and other academic officers if collective bargaining places them in roles that faculty members regard as antagonistic to faculty interests. The prospect of serious alienation of faculty and administration from one another as a result of the adversary relationship implicit in collective bargaining is a matter of concern. Equally important is the possible loss of much of the individual freedom and incentive that normally prevail in a noncollective or collegial campus setting.

Unionization of a college faculty usually comes in response to faculty grievances. Many of the objectives that faculty members seek through unionization can be achieved by the establishment of an effective internal grievance procedure that is easily accessible to faculty members, merits their confidence, and produces concrete and important results. A college administration that fails to face faculty grievances squarely thereby encourages the faculty to move toward unionization.

In any collective-bargaining situation, the college, like the union, has important assets and possible sanctions. For instance, salary demands can be met with demands for definite procedures of evaluation and accountability. The institution's response to collective bargaining may be to set specific productivity requirements, a move to which most faculties would justifiably object.

Where unions or other organizations are recognized as legal bargaining agents, both faculties and administrations should endeavor to conduct their negotiations in an atmosphere that will enhance rather than destroy the basic educational values which they both represent. This objective is more likely to be achieved if all concerned keep in mind the fact that American patterns of unionization and collective bargaining are traditionally oriented toward business and industry. It is possible that new patterns, such as third-party participation at various stages of the bargaining process, will be needed for bargaining in higher education in order to maintain both institutional diversity and shared responsibility and authority. In collective bargaining, moreover, special attention should be given to the need to protect the interests of students and the larger community.

Due Process on the Campus

Traditionally, the operation of colleges and universities has been characterized by informal understandings and policies developed and maintained through campus consensus. This consensus has grown fragile in recent years, and on many campuses it has been shattered. As a consequence, increasing numbers of institutions are defining extensive formal policies and procedures to govern relationships involving administration, faculty, and students. These developments, together with the growing inclination of individuals and groups to resort to legal action when they are aggrieved by institutional practices, are producing a "judicialization" of many campuses.

Increasing attention is also being given to the development of carefully written rules governing student, faculty, and staff conduct on the campus. All institutions should, with the assistance of competent legal counsel, establish judicially impeccable policies and procedures that guarantee due process in all matters affecting individual rights. Although there is danger that judicialized policies and procedures may reduce an institution's flexibility in responding to current problems, there are advantages in having predetermined guidelines when new problems arise. Where due process has been meticulously observed within an institution, the courts have usually been reluctant to intervene in its internal affairs.

Special efforts should be made by the president and his associates to encourage open lines of communication between the academic and the business elements of the institution, as well as between the administration and the faculty, the faculty and the students, and the students and the administration. Of special importance here is the trustees' access to knowledge of what is going on in the life of the campus and, in special cases, the faculty's access to the trustees. For this purpose, it is useful to consider such devices as general meetings of the faculty and the organization of elected faculty and student senates and executive committees to meet regularly with administrative officers in order to give advice and to share in decisions affecting institutional plans and priorities.

We strongly urge that all colleges and universities establish appropriate procedures of due process to guarantee the scrupulous observance of principles of justice and equity in all matters pertaining to faculty, students, and employees.

The judicialization of the campus is an added complication in college administration. It not only requires that college executives use extreme care in following formally established procedures, often with legal counsel, in carrying out their official duties. It also challenges them to cultivate a campus atmosphere in which personal human values are not submerged in a sea of mechanical and legal processes.

Chapter 6
A Strategy
for Better-Targeted
and Increased Financial Support

The funding gap facing the colleges can be attacked not only by better management of resources (as set forth in previous chapters) but also by securing more income from public and private sources. Earlier in this statement, we expressed our judgment that increased government support might be expected to match increased enrollment and increases in the cost of living and that such support per student in real terms would be maintained. If the cost of instruction per student continues to rise considerably faster than the cost of living, a funding gap will remain that can be met only from private sources. In this chapter, we review the pattern of financing for colleges and outline a strategy that can be expected to increase the resources available to the colleges and at the same time improve educational opportunity for students from lower-income families.*

In order to understand how the funding pattern can be improved, it is necessary to know what that pattern is. Funding for undergraduate education flows through various channels from four sources: students

---

*See Memoranda by MR. JOHN A. PERKINS, page 90, and MR. THEODORE O. YNTEMA, page 91.

and their families, state and local governments, the federal government, and gifts and endowments. These flows are traced in the Annex, which describes the financing system for the academic year 1969–70.

Families and students pay for nearly 60 per cent of all the costs associated with undergraduate education in the United States. By far the greater part of this expenditure is for food, housing, clothing, books, and other living expenses. These noninstructional costs constitute about 46 per cent of total expenditures for undergraduate education.

In developing a strategy for increasing financial support, we concentrate in this chapter on the instructional costs that account for the other 54 per cent of total expenditures for undergraduate education. These expenditures are funded largely (nearly 70 per cent) by government. State and local governments contribute nearly one-half of the monies used for undergraduate instructional purposes, and the federal government contributes about one-fifth. Parents and students finance about one-fifth of the expenditure. (However, on a gross basis, including government subsidies and allowances on behalf of students, parents and students pay two-fifths of the instructional bill through tuition and fees.) Gifts and endowment income fund approximately one-tenth of these costs. Although we believe that corporate and private giving should, and will, increase, the major source of increased support other than government is students and their parents.

This raises a central question. How should the costs of higher education be shared by society and individuals?

As we pointed out in discussing the basic purposes of higher education (Chapter 1), the benefits to society and the individual derived from undergraduate education are not mutually exclusive. It is clear that each gains both culturally and economically from higher education, with the benefits appearing to accrue chiefly to society in some instances and to individuals in others. The education of individuals should benefit society by the extension of knowledge and skill, the cultivation of greater social intelligence and cultural vitality, and increased economic productivity. At the same time, an individual may generally be expected to benefit by increased income and an improved quality of life.[1]

The problem of funding colleges and universities would be simple if it were possible to assign some values of higher education exclusively to

---

1/We are aware, of course, that the relationship between education and increased personal income is a matter of controversy.

the individual and the remainder to society. The student and his family would pay the cost for the individual benefits realized, while society would pay for the balance through government and corporate appropriations and gifts. But a precise division of values and costs in this regard is quite impossible.

Because higher education produces extensive social values, we do not recommend that all or even most students be required to pay the full cost of their schooling through tuition and fees. On the contrary, we advocate government subvention of both institutions and individuals. Nevertheless, because of the benefits of education to the individual, we consider it appropriate for students and their families to pay as large a part of the cost as they can afford.

Equalizing Opportunity by Grants to Students

We have raised the question of whether government support is effectively directed toward the goal of equalizing educational opportunity. We have found that to a marked degree those who stand in greatest need of assistance as college students because of disparities in family income are receiving a disproportionately small share of the support.

Analysis of how much government support is received by students from families with various income levels (see pages 79–80) shows that although government support has been greatest for low-income students, it has also been extensive for students from higher-income families. Moreover, support has been as great for students from higher-income families as for those from moderate-income families. With government support so distributed, it is not surprising to find that a college-age person from a family with annual income of $15,000 or more was almost five times more likely to be in college that one from a family with income of $3,000 or less. In our opinion, the present distribution of state and federal funding cannot bring about substantial improvement in the equality of opportunity in undergraduate education because aid is not concentrated on those who need it most. Moreover, as we shall show, correcting this faulty distribution of government aid by targeting it primarily to those who need it most can become a key factor in obtaining more resources for higher education.

We believe that the equalization of educational opportunity should be a major social goal and therefore a basic responsibility of government. State governments bear a large measure of the responsibility for in-state equalization, but general equalization extending beyond state systems is appropriately a task for the federal government.

Equality of educational opportunity can conceivably be achieved in several ways. College costs for students who could not otherwise enroll can be reduced through (1) general grants to institutions, whether based on enrollment or on some other criterion; (2) grants to institutions based specifically on enrollment of lower-income students; or (3) direct grants to lower-income students. Which funding mode will most efficiently support the goal of equalizing opportunity?

General grants to institutions, the most common form of aid, can result in any of the following: an increase in institutional quality without an increase in tuition, a general reduction in tuition for all students, or an institutionally administered selective reduction in tuition for lower-income students. Only if the latter result occurred would the advantage of public support be equitably distributed in terms of need. For this reason we prefer the method of direct aid to low-income students. It ensures that public resources will in fact lower the personal cost of college attendance for the grant recipients. A program of grants to lower-income students can effectively concentrate public resources on the goal of equality of educational opportunity and at the same time provide additional support for the colleges.

We wish to make it entirely clear that although we favor the use of public money to equalize educational opportunity, we are not advocating that colleges and universities lower or abandon their academic standards. On the contrary, an individual's eligibility for a grant should be tied to his or her admission to a qualified institution. Public funds should be made available only to those who can profit from postsecondary education, whether in a college, university, or vocational-technical school. Every institution should guard against the temptation to permit the pursuit of equal opportunity to endanger the quality of education.

Although federal funding practices should be more or less constant throughout the country, state practices may be expected to vary. In some states, for instance, the tradition of private education is stronger than it is in others. In these states, individual student grants from public money may be more acceptable to the taxpayer than they would be in states where most higher education takes place in state-owned and state-operated institutions. State-funded student grants may be more acceptable in the East and Middle West than in areas where there are comparatively few private colleges and universities, notably the Southwestern, Rocky Mountain, and Pacific regions.

We recommend that federal funding of undergraduate education be primarily through grants and loans to individual students in accordance with their ability to pay. We also recommend that funding patterns of state governments place more emphasis on grants and loans to students according to the same criterion. We further urge that wherever possible the federal government employ its undergraduate financial assistance in a manner which will contribute to more equal educational opportunity among the states. The unequal financial status of the states places this responsibility on the federal government.

Because tuition typically does not cover the full cost of education, we believe that direct student grants should be accompanied by institutional grants to cover a part of the additional cost incurred by the enrollment of students receiving grants. We recognize that the present and recent practice of the federal government in joining institutional grants to graduate fellowships and traineeships has proved its value, and we believe it should be extended to future undergraduate student-grant programs.

Coupling institutional grants with student grants has particular importance not only for technical colleges but also for community colleges, which train large numbers of paraprofessionals and technicians. Such technical and occupational training is more costly, often considerably so, than traditional undergraduate education. At present, these low-tuition technical and community colleges are a major force in the equalization of educational opportunity. It is therefore vitally important to assure their continuance by covering at least part of the added costs that result from both remedial and technical training. This by no means gainsays the urgent need to provide much greater opportunities for those who are economically disadvantaged to attend liberal arts colleges and universities.

Because of the increased cost of educating the economically disadvantaged, we recommend that institutions enrolling such persons holding government-supported grants and loans receive appropriate institutional grants.

Although government student grants should be made directly to the individual recipients (perhaps on the pattern of GI payments), thus leaving them free to select their schools, we believe that it would be advisable for the government to contract with colleges and universities to provide services in support of the grants program. Otherwise it may be necessary to create a large and expensive bureaucracy to administer the grants. The determining factors here should be effectiveness in achieving the goal of equality of educational opportunity and efficiency in administering the funds.

Enlarging the Student-Loan Program

As part of a more efficient use of government funds to support higher education, ample resources should be provided for loans to students to meet financial deficiencies from grants and from family resources. The student-loan market must ensure that youths from low- and moderate-income families, whose parents cannot contribute extensively (if at all) to their college education, will have access to capital. It may be detrimental to the academic success of these students to demand that they work extensively to finance a major share of their college expenses unless cooperative school-work programs operate at their institutions. Moreover, access to supplemental financial resources is also necessary to many middle- and upper-income families if they are to finance a greater share of college costs.

We recommend an expanded federally operated student-loan system to provide students and their families guaranteed access to supplemental funds. Past experience justifies continuing studies of loan programs and experimentation with structure and adminstration.

Although we are confident that middle- and upper-income groups can and will pay larger shares of college costs, it is unrealistic to require that all college expenses be paid out of current income and assets. Moreover, as college costs rise, the income level at which grants and loans are made available must also rise.

We recognize that both annual repayment levels and the risk involved in incurring large-scale, long-term debt may be important detriments to student borrowing. Furthermore, although loans are not unattractive alternatives to persons of typical middle-class economic experience, they may in other cases be formidable barriers to an education. This problem can probably be best handled by a loan program that permits (1) income-contingent repayments for low-income persons and (2) constant repayments for middle- and upper-income borrowers. Of course, there must be a limit on income-contingent loans to prevent overcommitment. Moreover, extended repayment terms should be possible, together with certain kinds of forgiveness features.*

Government-sponsored loan programs to supplement student grants put market restraints on both students and institutions that may in the long run benefit the quality of individual education by strengthening institutional management. Another important aspect of extensive loan programs is the implicit recognition of the increasing maturity and independence of college-age students.

Raising Low Tuition and Fees

The shift to increased federal funding through direct student grants and loans and increased emphasis on direct state aid to students, as opposed to institutional or institutionally administered programs, would alter considerably the support patterns and the tuition requirements of individual institutions. To the extent that this change achieves its objective, there would be an increase in the number of students from low-income families attending college. Because tuition income generally represents only a fraction of instructional cost, most colleges may not recapture (at present tuition levels) the whole of the institutional support they may have lost by the shift to funding through student grants and loans. Moreover, many of the disadvantaged students who would enroll under an expanded grant and loan program may require special instruction to remedy academic deficiencies, which would raise the cost of instruction. These adverse effects on colleges can be avoided by revising tuition charges. It should be emphasized that the shift from institutional to student grants and the increase in tuition are inseparable parts of the program.

The second part of our proposed strategy for increasing financial support for the colleges therefore calls for an increase in tuition charges where these are relatively low. They are, of course, generally low in

---

*See Memorandum by MR. WILLIAM M. ROTH, page 87.

public institutions. An increase in tuitions and fees would enable these colleges to recapture government aid from students receiving grants and, more importantly, to increase their income from students whose families are able to pay. The increase in tuition charges should be large enough to increase the total volume of resources available to the colleges.

We believe that tuition charges at many colleges and universities are unjustifiably low. We recommend an increase in tuitions and fees, as needed, until they approximate 50 per cent of instructional costs (defined to include a reasonable allowance for replacement of facilities) within the next five years. For two-year community colleges and technical colleges, we recommend that the increase be phased over ten years. Most of this increase may be expected to occur in the public sector.*

The recommendation that the suggested increase in the case of community and technical colleges be phased over ten years gives recognition to the special problems of this group of institutions. As previously noted, instruction at community colleges tends to be high cost because of the technical or professional nature of the training and also because of the large numbers of disadvantaged students enrolled. Time should be allowed for these institutions to create long-range plans for the effective use of resources, to develop special funding for needed programs, to reduce duplication and redundant courses and facilities, to make consortia arrangements, and to make similar managerial and organizational improvements suggested elsewhere in this statement.

The dollar amount of the increase suggested (averaging $540 a student in universities and four-year colleges) is in line with increases actually realized by private colleges in the decade of the 1960s. Moreover, even after the increase, the level of tuition at public four-year colleges would be only about one-half that of private four-year colleges.

Effects of Increasing Support Through Student Grants and Higher Tuition

If a policy of pricing tuition and fees at one-half of instructional costs had existed in the last decade, we estimate that the revenues of public undergraduate institutions in 1969–70 would have been increased

---
*See Memorandum by MR. HERMAN L. WEISS, page 87.

by nearly $1.7 billion. (This assumes that the program was five years old and that two-year community colleges and technical colleges had raised tuition by only one-half the difference between current tuition and 50 per cent of cost.) Not all of this increase would have been a net increment to the resources available to support colleges. Some of the increased tuition revenues would have been provided as student grants or loans to low- and moderate-income students to enable them to meet higher tuition costs. We estimate that approximately $600 million of $1.7 billion would have been utilized to meet tuition increases. As a result of the increase in direct support by the colleges for low- and moderate-income students, few, if any, of these students would have faced higher college costs as a result of the tuition increases. We estimate that government grants to low-income students would have exceeded the tuition increase for all students whose family income (in 1969–70) was less than $8,600. The government grant program would therefore have stimulated attendance by students from lower-income families (see Annex).

The effect of the proposed changes in government support could greatly reduce the proportion of institutional support received by the colleges from government (from 77.7 to 38 per cent) and greatly increase the proportion of government support received through student grants. Most important, of course, would be a net increase in annual college income of $1.1 billion, or 18 per cent, from private sources.

It is important to recognize that under our proposal the increases in tuition are intended not to precede but to follow or coincide with the availability of funds to the prospective students to pay that tuition. We are not proposing that institutions raise tuition under circumstances where the funds for that tuition will not be forthcoming.

The Committee is fully aware of the controversial nature, particularly within the academic community, of any recommendation to raise the tuitions of public institutions to approximately 50 per cent of instructional costs. We are aware also that to the extent that our recommendations produce shifts away from institutional funding they will incur considerable opposition. Several of the Subcommittee's nontrustee members and advisors and the project director have expressed their disagreement with these recommendations.* We would like to note here their dissent from the position on these matters taken by the trustees.

---

*See Memorandum by MR. ROBERT C. WEAVER, page 87.

Relating Institutional Support to Social Goals

We have stated our conviction that funding should be related to goals and that the goals of education can best be achieved by a combination of institutional and student support from government. The large task of extending equality of educational opportunity can best be achieved by increased student grants and loans as we have recommended. The other basic goals of education can best be achieved by institutional grants and appropriations because these require direct institutional action in establishing and maintaining instructional programs.

In considering patterns of funding, we are conscious of the economic, social, and political realities of the present institutional structure. We are concerned not with some ideal society but with this country and its institutions over the foreseeable future. Qualified institutions now in existence must be adequately funded if individual students are to receive the educational opportunities we believe they should have and if the needed social gains from higher education are to be realized. Although important changes in methods can be made, the nation's educational establishment or social and political conventions cannot be simply abolished or completely reconstructed.

There are important differences between public and private institutions, and funding by public money should respect those differences. Public institutions are subject to governmental control and are expected to respond to public interests in a number of ways, in such matters as admission and retention and through such programs as continuing education and certain kinds of public service. The land-grant colleges are an excellent example of tax-supported institutions that have traditionally served broad, publicly conceived social goals. A private liberal arts college, on the other hand, may prefer to concentrate its energies on a specialty with limited social interests.

It is appropriate that public colleges and universities receive a larger percentage of their income from tax monies than private institutions. Moreover, government grants to private institutions should take account of the income available to those institutions from private sources. Otherwise, those grants would generate disproportionate funding of private institutions that already have large incomes from nongovernmental funds. Private colleges and universities may be expected to continue to receive larger sums from private gifts than public institutions. In matters pertaining to religion, of course, funding with public money is subject to the law and court decisions.

We distinguish three major categories of funding that effectively relate the social goals of education to institutional support.

General-purpose grants. The acquisition of knowledge and the stimulation of learning occur throughout the college years in all types of programs and in all types of institutions. This is the basic purpose of every educational institution. Therefore, a funding program designed to achieve this goal should not be restricted to specific institutions or types of institutions or to specific academic fields; rather, it should provide resources on an equitable basis to those colleges and universities that are capable of producing quality education.

We believe that the most equitable basis for the distribution of such funds is the total student enrollment at all undergraduate levels because that enrollment is an index of institutional costs. We recognize that different types of institutions have differing patterns of nongovernmental support, that they incur different levels of cost (e.g., technical colleges as compared with liberal arts colleges), and that therefore differential institutional grants based on institutional type are warranted. We believe that since the education of an informed citizenry should be a basic function of every postsecondary institution (a function that we expect of every college and university), this goal should also be supported by general institutional grants.

We recommend the continuation of general-purpose grants and appropriations to institutions as the primary form of funding by state and local governments. The amount of these grants and appropriations should be based on undergraduate enrollment and type of undergraduate institution. They should be available to all types of public or tax-supported institutions.*

Categorical grants. We assume that it is advisable at various times for both federal and state legislatures to fund educational programs for achieving specific social objectives. Educational programs intended to satisfy professional and paraprofessional or other manpower demands are best served by categorical institutional grants designed to increase

---

*See Memorandum by MR. JOHN R. COLEMAN, page 91.

institutional quality and capacity in specific fields. Programs established in the past for such purposes as advancing science or improving space technology have been obviously successful. Now there are new needs—for example, in environmental management and other domestic areas affecting the quality of human life—where infusions of new resources are desirable. Today, few institutions can move into new educational programs, however valuable to society, without the new money that depends largely on categorical grants from federal and state or private sources.

We recommend a system of federal and state categorical grants to both public and private institutions to fund special educational programs designed to meet particular social objectives where those programs cannot be financed from regular budgets or private grants. We are especially conscious of the fact that some special programs (e.g., in advanced language and area studies) are of value to the nation as a whole, not simply to a single state or region, and that they therefore justify federal support.

Contractual arrangements. While some public institutions are overburdened with undergraduate students for whom they cannot provide adequate facilities and faculty, many private schools have space for additional students and in fact need more students to maintain their quality and meet their financial obligations. There are other situations in which considerations of economy indicate that private universities with long-established graduate and professional programs should make contractual arrangements with the state to expand their capacity and productivity rather than have the state duplicate them with new programs in public institutions.

It is clearly in the public interest in such instances to negotiate contracts that would supply public funds to private schools to enable them to enroll additional students and to carry on specified educational functions. Such arrangements can provide needed education at a financial saving to the public and at the same time contribute to the strength of private higher education.

We recommend that state and local governments contract with private colleges and universities to provide undergraduate, professional, and graduate education where public facilities are not adequate. In this way, underutilized private resources will be put to use instead of being duplicated at additional cost.*

---

*See Memorandum by MR. WILLIAM M. ROTH, page 88.

Strengthening Voluntary Support of Higher Education

Finally, in recognition of the importance of private gifts and grants as a source of institutional income, we believe that public policies aimed at encouraging private financial support of colleges and universities (both public and private) should be maintained and strengthened.

Prior to the establishment of the land-grant colleges and state universities, private funds of this character constituted the most important single source of income to higher education. As a result of the growth of governmental support in the last hundred years, private giving has declined in relative importance as a component of total income, and today it accounts for less than 10 per cent of all funds received by all undergraduate institutions (see Figure 3). For a majority of the institutions, however, gift income continues to be a vital element in the financing of undergraduate education.

We believe that the importance of voluntary support of higher education transcends its relative magnitude as a component of institutional funding. For many institutions, these funds provide a vital margin for educational quality. They have made possible buildings, grounds, equipment, and other facilities that are indispensable parts of the physical plants of colleges and universities and have financed the appointment of first-rank scholars and teachers. They have made possible scholarships, grants, and other forms of student aid that otherwise would not have been available. New instructional programs and techniques and curricular changes of critical importance to education would have been impossible without them. Moreover, they have supported special efforts in connection with the particular educational requirements of certain groups, such as women, racial minorities, rural communities, and those gifted in the arts, sciences, and humanities. Finally, for many private colleges and universities, these funds often make the difference between survival and extinction.

We have concluded that the flow of private support is essential to the diversity, strength, and vitality of the nation's colleges and universities. It provides a means of achieving the high degree of independence and freedom indispensable to the attainment and preservation of superior quality in education. We therefore conclude that the encouragement of private support is very much in the national interest.

It is clear that public policy in general and tax policy in particular influence the extent to which individuals, corporations, foundations, and other donors are willing and able to support higher education. We urge that this influence be explicitly recognized in the formulation and implementation of public policy so that it will have a maximum favorable impact on educational philanthropy.

Changes in tax policy and other matters related to philanthropic giving may be proposed for reasons not related to the problems of higher education, and these changes, if enacted, could well have an adverse impact on the levels of private support of higher education. Such a development would seriously compound the existing and prospective problems of college and university funding. Specifically, it would add greatly to the needs of both private and public colleges and universities for additional public funds, and this requirement could gravely complicate our recommendations for governmental programs of educational support.

In view of these considerations, **we urge that the existing tax incentives for voluntary support of higher education be maintained and, to the extent not incompatible with other objectives, expanded in order to strengthen the base of financial support of all colleges and universities.**

Annex: The Funding of Undergraduate Education

The following pages present a graphic and tabular treatment of the ways in which funds for undergraduate education have been raised and distributed and of how the patterns could be affected by CED's recommendations regarding tuition charges and government aid.

The first part of this presentation traces the flow of funds to undergraduate education from the chief sources of funding, both public and private. The second part shows how these funds have been distributed to individuals according to income level. In the third part, an attempt is made (1) to estimate the effects that CED's proposals could have on tuition levels at public institutions and (2) to illustrate the kinds of changes that might take place in governmental support if the suggested increase in direct student aid is implemented, including the impact this might have on students at different income levels.

Figure 3
Financing Undergraduate Education, 1969–70

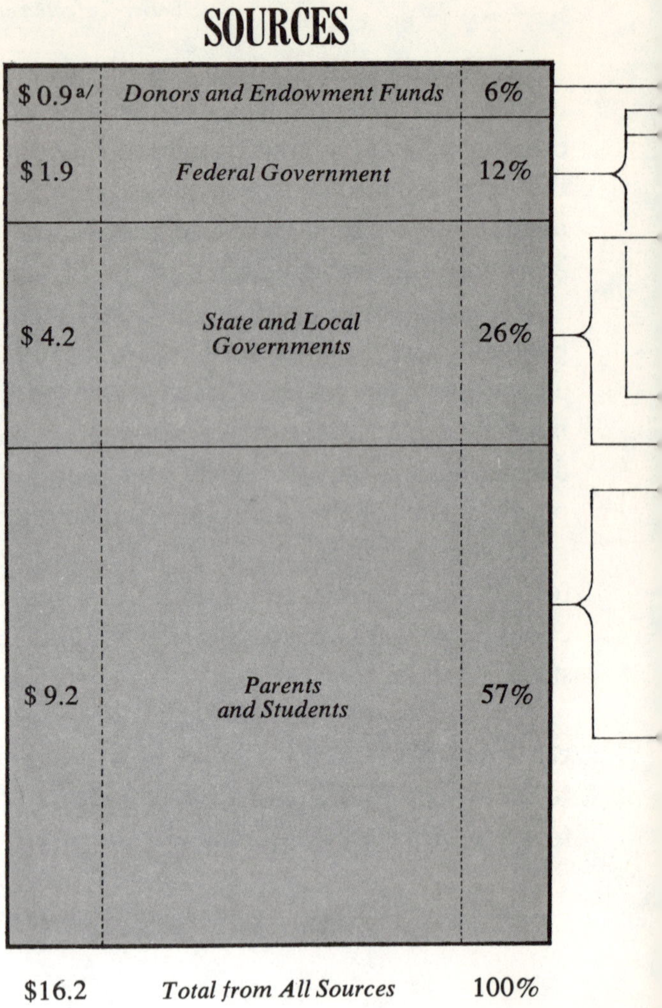

SOURCES

Amount	Source	Percent
$0.9 a/	Donors and Endowment Funds	6%
$1.9	Federal Government	12%
$4.2	State and Local Governments	26%
$9.2	Parents and Students	57%
$16.2	Total from All Sources	100%

(billions, not including capital expenditures)

Note: Figures may not total due to rounding.

Source: David S. Mundel, "The Cost of Higher Education, 1969–70 to 1979–80: An Estimate of Expenditures and Revenues," unpublished (March 1971).

How funds have been provided. The four major sources of funding for undergraduate education are students and parents, the federal government, state and local governments, and private donors and endowment funds. The totals shown above are the operating expenditures, both instructional and noninstructional, attributable only to undergraduate education in the academic year 1969–70. The portion of higher-education expenditures attributed to graduate education is not included. Nor does the data include capital expenditures or foregone student income.

Students and their families. In 1969–70, the cost of undergraduate living expenses to students and their families was $7.4 billion, more than twice as much as the $3.5 billion gross expenditure for tuition and fees. This indi-

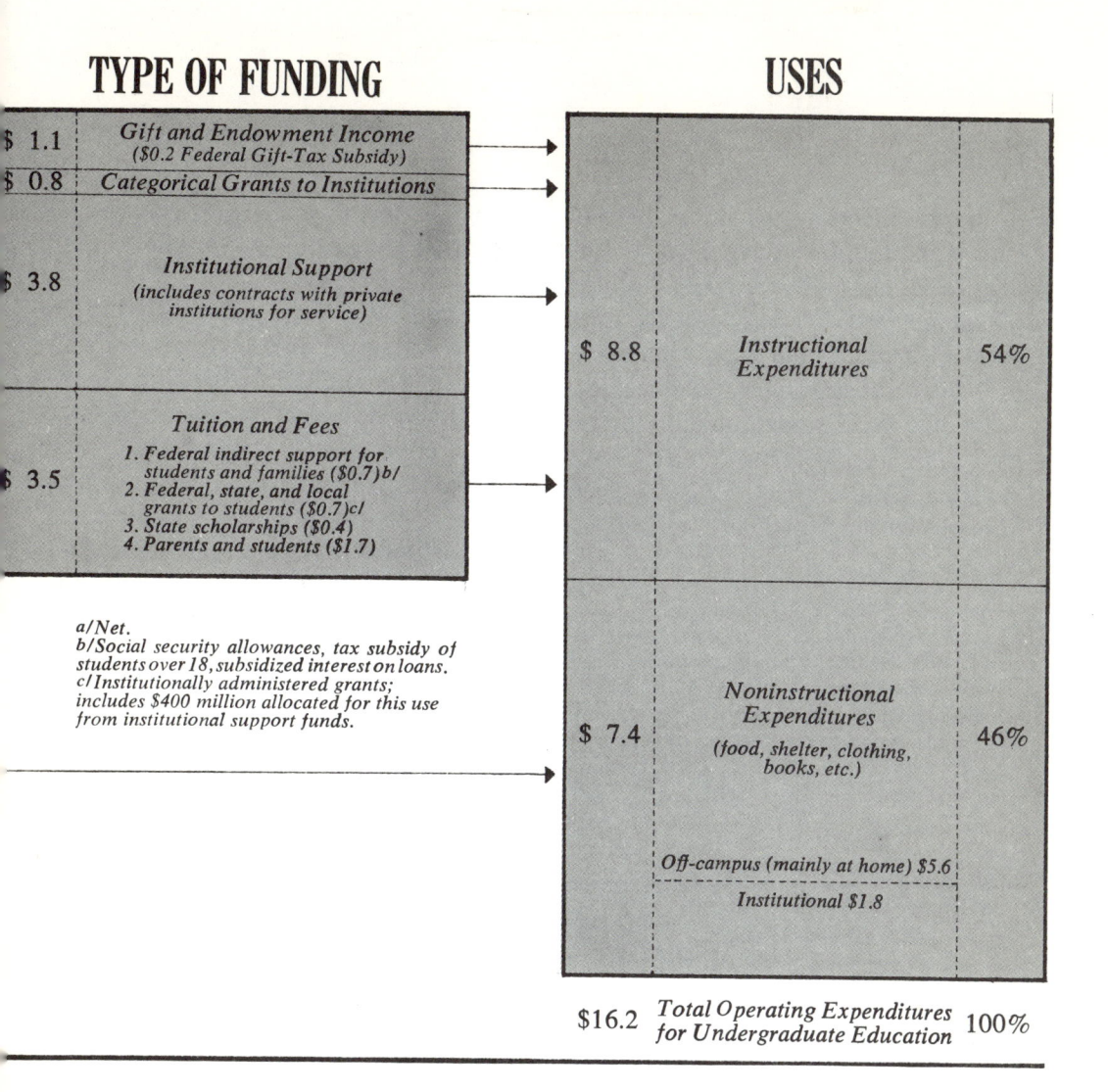

TYPE OF FUNDING		USES	
$ 1.1	Gift and Endowment Income ($0.2 Federal Gift-Tax Subsidy)		
$ 0.8	Categorical Grants to Institutions		
$ 3.8	Institutional Support (includes contracts with private institutions for service)	$ 8.8 — Instructional Expenditures	54%
$ 3.5	Tuition and Fees 1. Federal indirect support for students and families ($0.7)b/ 2. Federal, state, and local grants to students ($0.7)c/ 3. State scholarships ($0.4) 4. Parents and students ($1.7)		
		$ 7.4 — Noninstructional Expenditures (food, shelter, clothing, books, etc.)	46%
		Off-campus (mainly at home) $5.6 Institutional $1.8	
		$16.2 Total Operating Expenditures for Undergraduate Education	100%

a/Net.
b/Social security allowances, tax subsidy of students over 18, subsidized interest on loans.
c/Institutionally administered grants; includes $400 million allocated for this use from institutional support funds.

cates that being able to live at home may be more important than low or no tuition for many low-income students; this is particularly the case in community colleges and technical colleges.

As shown in Figure 3, students and their families received approximately $1.7 billion in tax and other subsidies from all levels of government, compared with the $9.2 billion they spent out of their own income, savings, and private borrowings. About $1 billion of the government aid was in the form of scholarships and institutionally administered student grants from federal, state, and local governments. The remaining $700 million was received through federal loan and tax subsidies and through the social security system. Loan subsidies give students the ability to borrow at less-than-market interest rates; tax subsidies permit the parents to count students as deductions beyond their eighteenth birthday.[1] Finally, student children of a deceased or disabled parent covered by social security receive benefits beyond their eighteenth birthday because of their student status.

Income that a student might earn on a job (instead of going to college) is not included in our estimates of costs. Such foregone earnings might be considered an investment yielding returns in the form of higher lifetime income.

State and local governments. In 1969–70, state and local governments provided a total of $4.2 billion for undergraduate education, of which some $3.8 billion was in the form of institutional support, mainly to public institutions. The institutions in turn allocated about $400 million of this money for student grants. In addition, state and local governments provided students about $400 million in direct scholarship aid. More recently, state and local governments have begun to contract for services from private institutions to provide education for students when public

---

[1]/Subsidies should not be confused with total flows. For example, loan subsidies are only a small fraction of total loans. In this categorization, work-study funds are considered support to institutions for necessary labor services; they count as wages and not as subsidies to the student.

**Table 1
Contribution to Total Costs of Undergraduate Education, by Source, Selected Income Groups, 1966–67**

Family Income	Federal[a]	State and local	Total
Under $4,000	$668	$808	$1,476 (63%)
$8,000–$10,000	296	793	1,089 (43%)
$15,000–$20,000	335	748	1,083 (40%)
$30,000 and over	383	517	900 (31%)

Note: Figures may not total due to rounding.

[a]/Federal support includes a small share of research funds that are assumed to subsidize undergraduate education.

facilities are overcrowded and private facilities have excess capacities. Public funds are paid to the private school for the students covered by such contracts.

The federal government. Including tax and other subsidies, federal aid to undergraduate education totaled about $1.9 billion in the school year 1969–70. Some $750 million of this was in the form of federal categorical support to institutions for undergraduate programs. Federal aid to graduate education, for research, and for construction was substantially more than this.

Federal aid to students included institutionally administered student grants of $300 million, social security allowances of $300 million, and loan subsidies of $165 million. Tax subsidies to students and their families amounting to some $200 million resulted from the tax-free status of scholarships and fellowships ($42 million) and the special treatment of student dependents ($166 million). Tax deductions on gifts to undergraduate institutions came to nearly another $200 million.

In passing the 1972 amendments to the Higher Education Act, Congress made a clear choice in favor of aid to students as opposed to aid to institutions as the means of promoting equality of educational opportunity. Likewise, it proposed to channel this increased student aid directly to the re-

Parental support	Student self-support	Total	Endowment and Gifts	Other	Total Cost per Student
72	$363	$ 435 (18%)	$127 (5%)	$305 (13%)	$2,343 (100%)
672	366	1,038 (40%)	145 (6%)	282 (11%)	2,564 (100%)
847	327	1,174 (44%)	190 (7%)	236 (9%)	2,683 (100%)
1,232	239	1,471 (51%)	308 (11%)	190 (7%)	2,869 (100%)

Families and Students columns: Parental support, Student self-support, Total.

Source: David S. Mundel and Sally H. Zeckhauser, "Who Pays the Higher Education Bill?" Prepared for Committee on Student Economics of the College Entrance Examination Board. Figures are based on U.S. Office of Education data and SCOPE data. (SCOPE—School to College: Opportunities for Post-Secondary Education—was a four-state study of 1966 high school graduates sponsored by the College Entrance Examination Board and the Center for Research and Development in Higher Education, University of California.)

cipients through the new Basic Opportunity Grants program, while the existing institutionally administered grant, loan, and work-study programs were to be reduced or replaced. However, this shift has not yet occurred. For fiscal 1974, the administration recommended that $622 million be appropriated for the opportunity-grants program and only $294 million for the older programs as compared with $781 million the year before. Instead, Congress reduced the opportunity-grant request to $122 million and funded the older programs at about the 1973 level.

The 1972 legislation also established the Student Loan Marketing Association (SLMA) to provide a secondary market for the federally guaranteed student-loan program. This is expected to make possible the extension of $1.6 billion in subsidized loans to another 1.5 million students, an increase of more than 50 per cent in the size of the program. The subsidies that permit students to borrow at less-than-market rates are of three kinds. The government (1) guarantees repayment without spreading the cost of default among other borrowers, (2) makes the entire interest payment while the student is in school if financial need can be shown, and (3) pays the bank or other lender the difference between 7 per cent and market rate (up to 3 per cent) for the remainder of the term of the loan.

Private gifts and endowments. In 1969–70, private gifts and endowments provided $1.1 billion toward undergraduate educational expenses (including the $200 million in tax deductions previously noted.)

How the funds have been distributed. Government assistance has not redressed inequities in educational opportunity resulting from unequal income. Funds have often been invested where least needed, and there has been a failure to correct fully the disparities in family income. This is clearly shown in Table 1. For example, students whose family income (1966–67) was between $15,000 and $20,000 received as much government support as those from families with an $8,000 to $10,000 income; students from some higher-income groups actually received *more* federal support than students from lower-income families did.

During the 1960s, income diminished slightly as a factor in determining college enrollment rates, but considerable gaps in opportunity remained between students from high- and low-income families. Lower-income students continued to be dramatically underrepresented on college campuses.

In 1970, six out of ten people eighteen to twenty-four years old from families earning more than $15,000 a year were in college. Only two out of ten in the same age group from families with incomes of $3,000 to $4,999 were in college. In 1970, a person eighteen to twenty-four years old from a family earning more than $15,000 was almost five times more likely to be in college than one in the same age group from a family with an income of under $3,000.

Table 2
Effects of Raising Public Institutions' Tuition and Fees to 50 Per Cent of Instructional Costs[a/]

	Universities	Four-Year Colleges	Two-Year Colleges
1. Estimated instructional costs per student in 1969-70	$1,992	$1,607	$1,226
2. Tuition and fees equal to 50 per cent of the cost	996	803	613
3. Average actual charges for tuition and fees in 1969-70	413	309	187
4. Increase in tuition and fees required to bring level up to 50 per cent of the cost[b/] (2 minus 3)	583	494	213[c/]

[a/] Costs here do not include depreciation.

[b/] Student support under categorical grant programs (e.g., for training paraprofessionals) would reduce these increases.

[c/] Because the recommendation suggests a ten-year phasing for two-year colleges, it is assumed here that only half the full recommended increase has been reached.

Sources: Instructional costs per student are based on estimates by June O'Neill, assuming an average 6 per cent annual inflation. Actual charges for tuition and fees are estimated in U.S. Office of Education, *Projections of Educational Statistics to 1980–81,* 1971 edition (Washington, D.C.: U.S. Government Printing Office, 1972).

How the CED recommendations would affect tuitions and government support. Most of the anticipated increase in tuition levels resulting from raising tuitions and fees would occur in the public institutions. As Table 2 shows, tuition and fees in public universities and colleges in 1969–70 averaged 20 per cent or less of instructional costs. For example, in four-year public colleges average tuitions and fees were only about $309 per full-time equivalent (FTE) student, as compared with an estimated average instructional cost of $1,607 for these students.

The dollar amount of the suggested increase, phased over a period of five years, averages $540 per student in universities and four-year colleges. This is in line with the increases actually realized by private colleges in the decade of the 1960s. The proposed level of tuition at public four-year colleges at the end of the five-year period would still average only half that of private four-year colleges. The tuition increase shown in Table 2 for two-year colleges is only half the full proposed amount because the recommendation urges that the increases for this group of institutions be phased over a ten-year period. Based on the undergraduate enrollment (FTE students) at that time, the levels of tuition shown here would have produced an additional $1.7 billion in revenues in 1969–70.

The Committee's proposals anticipate that part of the increased resources resulting from the recommended tuition increase would have to be used to provide student aid for low- and middle-income students. Indeed, if greater equality is to result from the Committee's recommendations, the student-grant program must provide lower- and moderate-income students with grants that exceed the recommended tuition changes. The greater the amount by which the grants exceed the tuition increases, the greater the stimulative effect of the grant program on enrollment.

The pattern of government support to colleges would be altered by shifting federal aid mostly to student grants and loans (except for some categorical grants to encourage high-priority undergraduate training) as well as by greater emphasis on grants and loans in state and local support. Table 3 (again using the 1969–70 data) illustrates the possible effect of such changes. Institutional support could drop from 77 per cent to between 38 and 63 per cent as a share of total government support (depending on how an optional 25 per cent is allocated). Therefore, those states that wish to continue heavy institutional support might approximate 64 per cent of aid in that form; states preferring the student-aid route might raise their proportion of such aid to 64 per cent.

The effect of the recommendations can be estimated by assuming that $2.3 billion in government support would have gone into student grants in 1969–70 had the recommended policies been instituted at that time. The $2.3 billion results from $1.0 billion in federal support and $1.3 billion of state and local support ($0.7 billion of the state support would come from the optional support category). Furthermore, it is assumed that all grants would go to students from families whose incomes were less than the median income for all college students. In 1969–70, this median income was approximately

Table 3
Effects of CED Recommendations on Government Support for Undergraduate Education *(based on 1969–70 school-year expenditure)*

Type of Government Support	Actual 1969-70 Expenditure	Proposed CED Recommen- dations	Change
	\multicolumn{3}{c}{billions of 1970 dollars}	
Federal			
Institutional			
Direct[a]	0.8	0.1	−0.7
Indirect	0.2	0.2	0.0
	1.0	0.3	−0.7
Undergraduate student			
Direct	0.3	1.0	0.7
Indirect[b]	0.7	0.7	0.0
	1.0	1.7	0.7
State and Local			
Institutional[c]	3.7	2.0	−1.7
Undergraduate student	0.4	0.6	0.2
Optional	—	1.5	1.5
	4.1	4.1	0.0
Total	6.1	6.1	0.0
	\multicolumn{3}{c}{per cent}	
All Levels of Government			
Institutional	77	38	−51
Student	23	38	64
Optional	—	25	—

[a] Categorical institutional aid.
[b] Student-loan and tax subsidies and social security payments.
[c] General support and contract programs.
Source: See Figure 3. Data may not be identical due to rounding.

$12,000. If the suggested pattern were followed, the maximum student grant would be $1,350 with a student-grant budget of $2.3 billion.

Students whose family incomes were below $8,000 (actually $8,600) would have grants exceeding the average tuition increases for all types of public institutions as shown in Table 3. Thus, the enrollment of these students would be positively stimulated by the policies recommended in this statement.

The stimulative effect of this program is illustrated in the following table:

Family income	Average grant amount
Below $ 4,000	$1,350
6,000	1,000
8,000	675
10,000	338
12,000	0

Note: The source of the data on which Figure 3 and the foregoing analysis are based is David S. Mundel, "The Cost of Higher Education, 1969–70 to 1979–80: An Estimate of Expenditures and Revenues" unpublished (March 1971). His extrapolations are derived from the following: June O'Neill, *Resource Use in Higher Education* (Berkeley: Carnegie Commission on Higher Education, 1971); U.S. Department of Health, Education, and Welfare, Office of the Assistant Secretary for Planning and Evaluation, *Health, Education, and Welfare Trends, 1966–67* (Washington, D.C.: U.S. Department of Health, Education, and Welfare, 1968); U.S. Office of Education, *Financial Statistics of Institutions of Higher Education: Current Funds, Revenues, and Expenditures, 1966–67* (Washington, D.C.: U.S. Government Printing Office, 1969); U.S. Office of Education, *Financial Statistics of Institutions of Higher Education: Student Financial Aid, 1966–67* (Washington, D.C.: U.S. Government Printing Office, 1969).

Memoranda of Comment, Reservation, or Dissent

Page 10—by THEODORE O. YNTEMA, with which CHARLES P. BOWEN, JR., JOHN R. COLEMAN, and LINCOLN GORDON have asked to be associated

I am not willing to accept the plea of labor intensiveness as an excuse for stagnant productivity in education. On the contrary, I believe there are opportunities for enormous improvements in productivity. These will, however, require a revolution in conventional academic views. If we could get faculties to subordinate their own special interests and really focus on what students need to learn and how they can best be helped to learn, we could establish a sound basis for improvement. Then colleges and universities could become institutions of higher *learning,* rather than places where students go to get course credits and degrees. If proper guides and learning materials were made available, much more responsibility for his education could be placed on the student. The energies that go into force-feeding and motivating students to learn facts and theories unimportant to them could be largely eliminated. The efforts of individual instructors to differentiate their own special courses could be reduced.

In another area, the frustrating pressures for research and publication on faculty members who cannot do original research should be eased or eliminated. At the same time, more research assistance should be given to those few who have special talents for it.

Page 17—by THEODORE O. YNTEMA, with which LINCOLN GORDON has asked to be associated

Operational specification of goals is especially important (and usually absent) in general education. University and college departments are organized by subject matter. The generally useful skills and abilities that students need to acquire are not the main interest of these departments. Most college teachers are specialists, and many of them do not have a good general education. As a result, much of what students are required to learn has little relevance or significance to their present or future lives. Only incidentally, if at all, do students acquire facility in the intellectual processes that they will need in their careers and other activities. The vested interests, the reward structure, and the traditions of the faculty make it almost impossible to develop appropriate programs of general liberal education. If the public does not rally to the support of general education, university and college faculties might do well to ask whether they deserve such support.

Page 17—by WILLIAM M. ROTH, with which JOSEPH L. BLOCK, CHARLES P. BOWEN, JR., JOHN R. COLEMAN, and LINCOLN GORDON have asked to be associated

This policy statement rightly emphasizes the need for diversity in higher education, including advanced work in various vocational areas. It should be pointed out, however, that American business and government both are to be faulted for using the undergraduate and, increasingly, the graduate degree as an easy and shorthand way of screening job applicants. Our culture still tends to regard four years of college, whether useful or not, as a necessary prelude to a successful career, much as nineteenth-century British leadership believed there was an evident relationship between high achievements in the classics and administrative abilities in the colonies.

Page 19—by ROBERT C. WEAVER

This, unfortunately, is not always true. A more accurate statement would be: "Elementary and secondary schools should provide the basic literacy and communication skills essential to good citizenship."

Page 25—by HERMAN L. WEISS

The equalization of educational opportunity among the states will help in lowering or removing the present additional tuition charges for out-of-state students. These additional charges seriously restrict the migration of students and thus deprive campuses of the opportunity to enroll a student body with diverse backgrounds and interests.

Pages 25 and 68—by WILLIAM M. ROTH, with which LINCOLN GORDON has asked to be associated

Although the general thrust of this analysis is probably correct, the student-loan recommendations are neither sufficiently comprehensive nor specific. For instance, the statement does not address the major financial problem faced by a middle-income family with several sons or daughters in college or indeed the increasing burden on lower-middle-income parents with only one university student to support. Neither do I understand why there "must be a limit on income-contingent loans to prevent over-commitment" if the goal of society is to extend higher education to all those who would benefit from it. In short, a CED statement on the financing of colleges should have made a more detailed proposal in these critical areas.

Pages 25 and 69—by HERMAN L. WEISS

Tuition and fees at private colleges and universities already are in excess of 60 per cent of instructional costs. If *publicly* supported institutions could increase *their* tuition and fees to the 50 per cent goal, private institutions would have an opportunity to attain even further increases where justified.

Pages 25 and 70—by ROBERT C. WEAVER

This recommendation has merit if viewed exclusively from the point of view of economic considerations. But colleges and universities, pressed as they are financially, cannot react solely to such considerations; recognition must be given to social and educational implications as well. Drastic increases in tuition in public institutions would frequently, if not always, occasion significant changes in the social and economic mix in student bodies as between private and public institutions. The impact would be greatest in those instances where current tuition is either nonexistent or very low. In these situations the imposition of tuition for the first time or significant increases in tuition would reduce the proportion of upper-income students in the public colleges and universities. Thus, I question the recommendation, especially the proposal to effect the changes over a period as short as five years.

Pages 26 and 73—by WILLIAM M. ROTH

This is an interesting and probably a sound idea, but I do not understand how it can be discussed without raising the church-state issue as it applies to religious colleges. No matter how justified from an economic point of view government assistance may be, there are legal and social questions that should not be swept under the desk.

Page 26—by HERMAN L. WEISS

There is a particular need to reexamine the provisions of the Tax Reform Act of 1969 insofar as gifts in kind are concerned. The limiting of tax credits for gifts of equipment or other products to the manufacturing cost of such items instead of the previous fair market value has led to a severe reduction in such gifts to the detriment of colleges and universities that had enjoyed such largesse for decades.

Page 32—by HERMAN L. WEISS, with which CHARLES P. BOWEN, JR., has asked to be associated

This entire paragraph is out of phase with the concept of "effective educational planning" being espoused. One cannot "develop both practical objectives and strategies for achieving those objectives within the framework of the institution's mission and basic goals" and then allow individual faculty members "a considerable degree of independence . . . in determining their own courses of instruction." The latter will work only if the degree of freedom and independence is within boundaries defined in the statement of mission, objectives, and goals.

Page 39—by JOSEPH L. BLOCK

Although I do not disagree with the comments on the possible favorable and unfavorable impacts of state coordinating (and planning) boards, it seems to me that the statement is remiss in not emphasizing adequately the important role that such bodies can and should play in higher education. In fact, I believe it damns them with faint praise.

In its recommendation, the statement only makes the point that these agencies should "not raise obstacles to diversity." Obviously, everyone could subscribe to that. But the statement should amplify, far more than it does, the strong positive force for effectiveness, efficiency, and innovation that a state planning and coordinating board can be.

Surely such an agency should develop and update long-range master plans for state systems. And, of course, this should be done in collaboration with all concerned institutions. It should serve as a catalytic agent for constructive change and, among other functions, stimulate the accomplishment of the desirable objectives set forth in this statement. For instance, it should be deeply involved in such matters as institutional missions and goals (pages 21 and 32); their growth, size, and cooperative ventures (pages 23 and 55); and the exploration and encouragement of nontraditional methods of education (pages 23 and 52).

Indeed, as far as large state systems are concerned, only through such leadership can waste, duplication, and inefficiency be minimized and diversity preserved. The statement should have called for the creation of coordinating boards in states where they do not exist and for the clarification of their functions, if necessary, where they do exist.

Page 48—by JOHN R. COLEMAN

Except in the financing section, our entire report suffers from a vagueness that may limit the effectiveness of its exhortations. Here the vagueness also carries potential for harm. To repeat as an example of waste the charge that faculty members spend too little time teaching, without any further elaboration, is mischievous. Until we are prepared to talk about norms or, better, to recognize a healthy diversity in the ways faculty members utilize their time on the college's behalf, we make no contribution to an effective attack on the waste that does exist but that is not measured by the hours spent in class.

Page 51—by JOHN R. COLEMAN, with which LINCOLN GORDON and C. WREDE PETERSMEYER have asked to be associated

This thought might be made more useful by including the possibility that some people may take a longer time to get their degrees and others may take a shorter time. We ought to encourage all students to consider the possibility of time off to work or to travel either before they come to college or during their college years. We ought to encourage more people who passed up college at the age of eighteen to consider it at the age of twenty-eight. And if we are serious about using educational resources wisely, we ought to encourage many students not to go to college at all. That, in turn, will require our giving more esteem than we do now to life patterns and careers for which college as we know it is poor preparation.

Page 53—by HERMAN L. WEISS

A major value of cooperative work-study programs is that they aid students to make the necessary cultural adjustment for entering a field of work where few, if any, role models have existed in the past. This is particularly true where they assist women and minority-group members to adjust to working conditions in fields such as engineering, accounting, and finance and in similar professions in which very few of their peers are presently employed.

Page 57—by ELLERY SEDGWICK, JR., with which C. WREDE PETERSMEYER has asked to be associated

I cannot agree with this paragraph. I would substitute: "Faculty tenure at one time was generally regarded as necessary for guaranteeing academic freedom. Under present-day circumstances, this safeguard is no longer required, and it tends to serve only as a symbol of rank and to shield incompetence or indolence."

Page 58—by JOHN R. COLEMAN

Here, at one of the few points where we are specific in our report, we offer no evidence to back up the fifty-fifty rule. At a minimum, we should recognize that one high cost of saying to younger faculty members that the tenured slots are filled is that they will focus their attention more on making reputations in their fields at large, principally through publications, than on doing first-class teaching jobs. If they know how academic markets work, they are all too aware that their teaching will be lightly evaluated by the institution to which they may go.

Page 62—by JOHN A. PERKINS

I must dissent from the general thrust of Chapter 6. It reflects primarily a concern for financing private higher education. Important as that segment is, it enrolls only slightly more than a quarter of the undergraduates in four-year institutions. The continued well-being of quality public higher education, which has made tremendous contributions through teaching, research, and public service (especially in the Middle West, South, and Far West), cannot but be adversely affected by the proposals set forth in this chapter. The strategy also seems to favor upper-income and disadvantaged families with young people aspiring to college education to the neglect of middle-income families, which pay a disproportionate share of the generally regressive state taxes and will be expected to educate their own children with a minimum of grants.

Present practice indicates a clear willingness of major public institutions to use student loans as one means of financing higher education. There are two issues that need much more extensive consideration than has been given them in this chapter. First, what proportion of costs for differently circumstanced students should be met by loans? This question is closely related to what proportion of true costs should come from charges to students in public institutions. Second, how likely are such loans to be collectable? Both the equitable loaning of funds and their satisfactory collection on schedule are certain to require large educational and governmental bureaucracies, the cost of which might better go directly into education. If loans must be extensively relied upon to finance the college experience, many young people will be discouraged from seeking the broad, liberal education commonly heralded by business leaders as most appropriate. Many others will be diverted to training programs that will guarantee a quick return on their educational investment in spite of the likelihood that such vocational training will become obsolescent long before they retire.

Page 62—by THEODORE O. YNTEMA

The value of education to society is very great indeed, but at the margin, increments of higher education are probably not worth much to society (excluding, of course, the benefits captured directly by the student). If this be so, there are good economic and social reasons for reducing the subsidies to higher education and for raising tuition rates and increasing the availability of student loans and of grants to neediest students. In addition, the side effects of such actions are likely to be good: more student power via tuition payments and more student concern and demand for improvement in education.

Page 72—by JOHN R. COLEMAN, with which CHARLES P. BOWEN, JR., and C. WREDE PETERSMEYER have asked to be associated

Our boldest recommendation in this report is the one emphasizing aid directly to students as a way to channel help where it can achieve the most social good and as a way to stimulate colleges to take their students more seriously (page 66). That controversial recommendation, with which I heartily agree, is undercut when we ask for institutional general-purpose grants, too. I see heavy wastes of public funds if we go the road of making grants to institutions of higher education just because they exist. At a minimum, surely, we should require some sort of college grants commission that would seek to measure the college's progress *toward its own stated goals* before any general grant is made. But I, for one, would prefer to see no such grants because they will perpetuate mediocrity in prestigious and struggling institutions alike, will encourage complacency, and will introduce government too deeply into private colleges.

Appendix
Research Papers on the Management and Financing of Colleges

A number of papers written by advisors and others associated with this project were studied by the Subcommittee on the Management and Financing of Colleges and the Task Force on Alternate Sources of College Funding in the course of their deliberations. These papers are listed below in two groupings.

1. Financing Higher Education

Aspects of a Voucher Plan for Higher Education, *Henry M. Levin, Stanford University*

Federal Aid to Higher Education: An Analysis of Federal Subsidies to Undergraduate Education, *David S. Mundel, Harvard University* (originally published in The Economics of Federal Subsidy Programs, part 4, a compendium of papers submitted to the Joint Economic Committee, August 28, 1972)

Federal Support for Higher Education: Policy Alternatives and Implications, *D. Bruce Johnstone, University of Pennsylvania*

The Financial Condition of Institutions of Higher Education and the Expenditures That Brought Them to It, *William W. Jellema, Potomac, Maryland*

The Goals of Higher Education and Their Financial Implications, *Howard R. Bowen, Claremont University Center*

Higher Education: Who Should Pay the Bill? *Ralph K. Huitt, National Association of State Universities and Land-Grant Colleges*

The Impact of Federal and State Policies on the Efficiency of Prices in Higher Education, *Robert W. Hartman, Brookings Institution*

Through Institutions or Through Students: The Current Dilemma in the Finance of American Higher Education, *Larry L. Leslie, Pennsylvania State University*

Tuition and the Costs of Higher Education, *Marc Nerlove, University of Chicago* (originally published in Journal of Political Economy, May/June 1972)

Who Pays the Higher Education Bill?, *David S. Mundel and Sally H. Zeckhauser, Harvard University*

2. The Management of Colleges

Accountability and Governance in the Seventies, *Kenneth P. Mortimer, Pennsylvania State University*

Cooperative Education and Financing Higher Education, *Asa S. Knowles, Northeastern University*

The Courts, Government, and Higher Education, *Robert M. O'Neil, University of Cincinnati* (originally published as CED Supplementary Paper Number 37, 1972)

Expanding Government, Shrinking Autonomy, and Governance, *John J. Corson, Fry Consultants Incorporated*

Facing Up to the Realities of Financing Higher Education, *David H. Kurtzman, University of Pittsburgh*

Faculty Unions and University Management, *Joseph W. Garbarino, University of California (Berkeley)*

Financial Management of Public Community Colleges, *Clyde E. Blocker, Harrisburg Area Community College*

The Governance of Community Colleges with Implications for their Management and Support, *Leland L. Medsker, University of California (Berkeley)*

The Impact of a State Board of Higher Education Upon College Management and Finance, *John D. Millett, Academy of Educational Development*

Improving the Quality of Instruction, *Kenneth E. Eble, University of Utah*

Long-Range Planning and Budgeting at Colleges and Universities, *Sidney G. Tickton and Alvin C. Eurich, Academy for Educational Development*

Nontraditional Financing of Colleges, *Robert H. Nelson, Robert H. Nelson & Associates*

Objectives and Goals: Their Role in the Governance of Colleges, *John J. Corson, Fry Consultants Incorporated*

Optimum Institutional Size: A Case of Conflicting Views, *Larry L. Leslie, Pennsylvania State University*

The Presidency: Leadership with Marginal Authority, *Thomas R. McConnell, University of California (Berkeley)*

Sense and Nonsense Regarding Accountability in Higher Education, *Rodney T. Hartnett, Educational Testing Service*

A Structure for University Administration, *Ronald W. Brady, Syracuse University*

The Tenure System in American Higher Education: Practices, Policies, and Alternatives, *Arvo Van Alstyne, University of Utah*

Unconventional Approaches to Postsecondary Education with Implications for Management and Support, *Leland L. Medsker, University of California (Berkeley)*

Task Force on Alternate Sources of College Funding

Chairman
*HARRY W. KNIGHT, President
Hillsboro Associates, Inc.

Co-chairman and Study Director
DAVID S. MUNDEL
John F. Kennedy School of Government
Harvard University

EARL F. CHEIT
Officer in Charge
Higher Education and Research
The Ford Foundation

ARLAND F. CHRIST-JANER, President
College Entrance Examination Board

JOSEPH P. COSAND, Director
Center for the Study of Higher Education
University of Michigan

CURTISS E. FRANK
Chairman, Executive Committee
Council for Financial Aid
   to Education, Inc.

KURT M. HERTZFELD, Treasurer
Amherst College

ROGER W. HEYNS, President
American Council on Education

HAROLD HOWE II, Vice President
Division of Education and Research
The Ford Foundation

RALPH K. HUITT, Executive Director
National Association of State
   Universities and Land-Grant Colleges

WILLIAM W. JELLEMA
Potomac, Maryland

D. BRUCE JOHNSTONE
Executive Assistant to the President
University of Pennsylvania

LARRY L. LESLIE
Research Associate, Center for the
   Study of Higher Education and
Chairman, Higher Education Program
The Pennsylvania State University

HENRY M. LEVIN, Associate Professor
School of Education
Stanford University

JOHN R. MEYER, President
National Bureau of Economic
   Research, Inc.

SAMUEL M. NABRIT
Executive Director
The Southern Fellowship Fund

JAMES NELSON
Vice President for Financing
   Higher Education
College Entrance Examination Board

MARC NERLOVE
Department of Economics
University of Chicago

GEORGE PETERSON
Research Staff
The Urban Institute

ROGER J. VOSKUYL
Executive Director
The Council for the Advancement
   of Small Colleges

ELIZABETH H. WHEELER
Former Secretary of Hampshire College

*CED Trustee

CED Board of Trustees

See pages 5 and 6 for list of Research and Policy Committee and the Subcommittee members who are responsible for the conclusions in this particular study.

Chairman
EMILIO G. COLLADO
Executive Vice President
Exxon Corporation

Vice Chairmen
WILLIAM H. FRANKLIN, Chairman
Caterpillar Tractor Co.
JOHN D. HARPER, Chairman
Aluminum Company of America
ROBERT B. SEMPLE, Chairman
BASF Wyandotte Corporation

Treasurer
WALTER W. WILSON, Partner
Morgan Stanley & Co.

E. SHERMAN ADAMS
Senior Vice President and Economist
The Fidelity Bank
O. KELLEY ANDERSON
Chairman, Executive Committee
Real Estate Investment Trust of America
ROBERT O. ANDERSON, Chairman
Atlantic Richfield Company
ERNEST C. ARBUCKLE, Chairman
Wells Fargo Bank
SANFORD S. ATWOOD, President
Emory University
BERNHARD M. AUER
Greenwich, Connecticut
JERVIS J. BABB
Wilmette, Illinois
CHARLES F. BARBER, Chairman
American Smelting and Refining Company
ROBINSON F. BARKER, Chairman
PPG Industries, Inc.
JOSEPH W. BARR, Chairman
American Security and Trust Company
HARRY HOOD BASSETT, Chairman
First National Bank of Miami
WILLIAM M. BATTEN, Chairman
J. C. Penney Company, Inc.
WILLIAM O. BEERS, Chairman
Kraftco Corporation
CECIL M. BENADOM, President
Beneficial Corporation
GEORGE F. BENNETT, President
State Street Investment Corporation
HAROLD H. BENNETT
Salt Lake City, Utah
JAMES F. BERE, President
Borg-Warner Corporation
JOSEPH L. BLOCK
Former Chairman
Inland Steel Company
W. MICHAEL BLUMENTHAL
Chairman and President
The Bendix Corporation
H. M. BOETTINGER
Director of Corporate Planning
American Telephone & Telegraph Company
CHARLES P. BOWEN, JR., Chairman
Booz, Allen & Hamilton Inc.
MARVIN BOWER, Director
McKinsey & Company, Inc.
R. MANNING BROWN, JR., Chairman
New York Life Insurance Co., Inc.
DANIEL P. BRYANT, Chairman
Bekins Company
JOHN L. BURNS, President
John L. Burns and Company
FLETCHER L. BYROM, Chairman
Koppers Company, Inc.
EDWARD E. CARLSON, President
United Air Lines
ROBERT J. CARLSON
Senior Vice President
Deere & Company
RAFAEL CARRION, JR.
Chairman and President
Banco Popular de Puerto Rico

EDWARD W. CARTER, Chairman
Broadway-Hale Stores, Inc.
JOHN B. CAVE, Senior Vice President
White Weld & Co., Incorporated
HUNG WO CHING, Chairman
Aloha Airlines, Inc.
W. GRAHAM CLAYTOR, JR., President
Southern Railway System
CATHERINE B. CLEARY, President
First Wisconsin Trust Company
JOHN R. COLEMAN, President
Haverford College
EMILIO G. COLLADO
Executive Vice President
Exxon Corporation
C. W. COOK, Chairman
General Foods Corporation
STEWART S. CORT, Chairman
Bethlehem Steel Corporation
ROBERT C. COSGROVE, Chairman
Green Giant Company
GEORGE S. CRAFT
Chairman, Executive Committee
Trust Company of Georgia
JOSEPH F. CULLMAN, 3rd, Chairman
Philip Morris Incorporated
JOHN H. DANIELS, Chairman
Independent Bancorporation
*DONALD K. DAVID
New York, New York
ARCHIE K. DAVIS, Chairman
Wachovia Bank & Trust Co.
R. HAL DEAN, Chairman
Ralston Purina Company
WILLIAM N. DERAMUS, III
Chairman and President
Kansas City Southern Industries, Inc.
JOHN DIEBOLD, Chairman
The Diebold Group, Inc.
LOWELL S. DILLINGHAM, Chairman
Dillingham Corporation
DOUGLAS DILLON
Chairman, Executive Committee
Dillon, Read and Co., Inc.
ROBERT R. DOCKSON, President
California Federal Savings
  and Loan Association
B. R. DORSEY, Chairman
Gulf Oil Corporation
CHARLES E. DUCOMMUN, President
Ducommun Incorporated
ALFRED W. EAMES, JR., Chairman
Del Monte Corporation
W. D. EBERLE
Special Representative for Trade Negotiations
Executive Office of the President
WILLIAM S. EDGERLY
Financial Vice President
Cabot Corporation
DANIEL F. EVANS, President
L. S. Ayres & Co.
WALTER A. FALLON, President
Eastman Kodak Company
RICHARD C. FENTON, President
Cooper Laboratories International, Inc.
FRANCIS E. FERGUSON, President
Northwestern Mutual Life Insurance Company
JOHN H. FILER, Chairman
Aetna Life and Casualty Company
WILLIAM S. FISHMAN, President
ARA Services, Inc.
E. B. FITZGERALD, Chairman
Cutler-Hammer, Inc.
*MARION B. FOLSOM
Rochester, New York
ROBERT T. FOOTE
Chairman and President
Universal Foods Corporation
CHARLES W. L. FOREMAN
Vice President
United Parcel Service
LAWRENCE E. FOURAKER
Dean, Graduate School of Business
  Administration, Harvard University

*Life Trustee

JOHN M. FOX, President
H. P. Hood Inc.
DAVID L. FRANCIS, Chairman
Princess Coal Sales Company
WILLIAM H. FRANKLIN, Chairman
Caterpillar Tractor Co.
GAYLORD FREEMAN, Chairman
The First National Bank of Chicago
DON C. FRISBEE, Chairman
Pacific Power & Light Company
CLIFTON C. GARVIN, JR., President
Exxon Corporation
LELAND B. GEHRKE
Group Vice President
3M Company
RICHARD L. GELB, President
Bristol-Myers Company
CARL J. GILBERT
Dover, Massachusetts
HUGH M. GLOSTER, President
Morehouse College
W. RICHARD GOODWIN, President
Johns-Manville Corporation
KERMIT GORDON, President
The Brookings Institution
LINCOLN GORDON
Fellow, Woodrow Wilson International
Center for Scholars
KATHARINE GRAHAM, Chairman
The Washington Post Company
JOHN D. GRAY, Chairman
Hart Schaffner & Marx
JOHN D. GRAY, Chairman
Omark Industries, Inc.
JOSEPH GRIESEDIECK, Vice Chairman
Falstaff Brewing Corporation
WALTER A. HAAS, JR., Chairman
Levi Strauss and Co.
TERRANCE HANOLD, President
The Pillsbury Company
R. V. HANSBERGER
Boise, Idaho
JOHN D. HARPER, Chairman
Aluminum Company of America
SHEARON HARRIS
Chairman and President
Carolina Power & Light Company
WILLIAM E. HARTMANN, Partner
Skidmore, Owings & Merrill
ROBERT S. HATFIELD, Chairman
Continental Can Company, Inc.
GABRIEL HAUGE, Chairman
Manufacturers Hanover Trust Company
H. J. HAYNES, President
Standard Oil Company of California
H. J. HEINZ, II, Chairman
H. J. Heinz Company
JAMES M. HESTER, President
New York University
JAMES T. HILL, JR.
New York, New York
*PAUL G. HOFFMAN
New York, New York
GEORGE F. JAMES
Cos Cob, Connecticut
WILLIAM M. JENKINS, Chairman
Seattle-First National Bank
RUSS M. JOHNSON, Chairman
Deposit Guaranty National Bank
SAMUEL C. JOHNSON, Chairman
S. C. Johnson & Son, Inc.
WILLIAM B. JOHNSON, Chairman
Illinois Central Industries, Inc.
GILBERT E. JONES
Senior Vice President
IBM Corporation
EDWARD R. KANE, President
E. I. du Pont de Nemours & Company
CHARLES KELLER, JR., President
Keller Construction Corporation
DONALD M. KENDALL, Chairman
PepsiCo, Inc.
JAMES R. KENNEDY, Vice Chairman
Celanese Corporation

CHARLES KIMBALL, President
Midwest Research Institute
PHILIP M. KLUTZNICK
Chairman, Executive Committee
Urban Investment and Development Co.
HARRY W. KNIGHT, President
Hillsboro Associates, Inc.
R. HEATH LARRY, Vice Chairman
United States Steel Corporation
RALPH LAZARUS, Chairman
Federated Department Stores, Inc.
RALPH F. LEACH
Chairman, Executive Committee
Morgan Guaranty Trust Co. of New York
FLOYD W. LEWIS, President
Middle South Utilities, Inc.
ROBERT D. LILLEY, President
American Telephone & Telegraph Company
FRANKLIN A. LINDSAY, President
Itek Corporation
LEONOR F. LOREE, II
Vice Chairman
The Chase Manhattan Bank
OSCAR A. LUNDIN
Executive Vice President
General Motors Corporation
J. EDWARD LUNDY
Executive Vice President
Ford Motor Company
J. PAUL LYET, Chairman
Sperry Rand Corporation
ROBERT P. LYNN
Senior Vice President
Burlington Industries, Inc.
*THOMAS B. McCABE
Chairman, Finance Committee
Scott Paper Company
C. PETER McCOLOUGH, Chairman
Xerox Corporation
THOMAS M. McDANIEL, JR., President
Southern California Edison Co.
GEORGE C. McGHEE
Washington, D.C.
JOHN G. McLEAN, Chairman
Continental Oil Company
E. L. McNEELY, President
The Wickes Corporation
RAY W. MACDONALD, President
Burroughs Corporation
IAN MacGREGOR, Chairman
American Metal Climax, Inc.
DONALD S. MacNAUGHTON, Chairman
Prudential Insurance Co. of America
MALCOLM MacNAUGHTON, Chairman
Castle & Cooke, Inc.
G. BARRON MALLORY
Jacobs Persinger & Parker
ROBERT H. MALOTT, Chairman
FMC Corporation
AUGUSTINE R. MARUSI
Chairman and President
Borden Inc.
WILLIAM F. MAY, Chairman
American Can Company
OSCAR G. MAYER
Chairman, Executive Committee
Oscar Mayer & Co.
H. TALBOTT MEAD
Chairman, Finance Committee
The Mead Corporation
CHAUNCEY J. MEDBERRY, III, Chairman
Bank of America N.T. & S.A.
EDWIN B. MEISSNER, JR.
Senior Vice President
General Steel Industries, Inc.
LOUIS W. MENK, Chairman
Burlington Northern, Inc.
CHARLES A. MEYER
Vice President and Director
Sears, Roebuck & Co.
ARJAY MILLER
Dean, Graduate School of Business
Stanford University
ROBERT R. NATHAN, President
Robert R. Nathan Associates, Inc.

*Life Trustee

ALFRED C. NEAL, President
Committee for Economic Development
ISIDORE NEWMAN, II, President
City Stores Company
J. WILSON NEWMAN
Chairman, Finance Committee
Dun & Bradstreet, Inc.
EDWARD N. NEY, President
Young & Rubicam International Inc.
JOHN O. NICKLIS, Chairman
Pitney-Bowes Inc.
DAVID PACKARD, Chairman
Hewlett-Packard Company
EDWARD L. PALMER
Chairman, Executive Committee
First National City Bank
RUSSELL E. PALMER
Managing Partner
Touche Ross & Co.
HENRY G. PARKS, JR.
President and Chairman
H. G. Parks, Inc.
DONALD S. PERKINS, Chairman
Jewel Companies, Inc.
JOHN A. PERKINS
Vice President—Administration
University of California, Berkeley
JOHN H. PERKINS, President
Continental Illinois National Bank
 and Trust Company of Chicago
HOWARD C. PETERSEN, Chairman
The Fidelity Bank
C. WREDE PETERSMEYER
Chairman and President
Corinthian Broadcasting Corporation
PETER G. PETERSON, Chairman
Lehman Brothers, Inc.
RUDOLPH A. PETERSON, Administrator
United Nations Development Program
THOMAS L. PHILLIPS, President
Raytheon Company
CHARLES J. PILLIOD, JR., President
The Goodyear Tire & Rubber Company
JOHN B. M. PLACE
Chairman and President
The Anaconda Company
DONALD C. PLATTEN, Chairman
Chemical Bank
GEORGE PUTNAM, Chairman
The Putnam Management Company, Inc.
R. STEWART RAUCH, JR., Chairman
The Philadelphia Saving Fund Society
PHILIP D. REED
New York, New York
JAMES Q. RIORDAN
Senior Vice President, Finance
Mobil Oil Corporation
MELVIN J. ROBERTS, Chairman
Colorado National Bank of Denver
JAMES E. ROBISON
Chairman, Finance Committee
Indian Head Inc.
AXEL G. ROSIN, Chairman
Book-of-the-Month Club, Inc.
WILLIAM M. ROTH
San Francisco, California
JOHN SAGAN
Vice President-Treasurer
Ford Motor Company
CHARLES J. SCANLON, Vice President
General Motors Corporation
HENRY B. SCHACHT, President
Cummins Engine Company, Inc.
THEODORE SCHLESINGER
Chairman, Executive Committee
Allied Stores Corporation
JOHN A. SCHNEIDER, President
CBS Broadcast Group
LEO H. SCHOENHOFEN, Chairman
Marcor, Inc.
D. C. SEARLE
Chairman, Executive Committee
G. D. Searle & Co.
ELLERY SEDGWICK, JR., Chairman
Medusa Corporation

RICHARD B. SELLARS, Chairman
Johnson & Johnson Worldwide
ROBERT B. SEMPLE, Chairman
BASF Wyandotte Corporation
MARK SHEPHERD, JR., President
Texas Instruments Incorporated
LEON SHIMKIN, President
Simon and Schuster, Inc.
RICHARD R. SHINN, President
Metropolitan Life Insurance Company
ROCCO C. SICILIANO, President
The TI Corporation
GRANT G. SIMMONS, JR., Chairman
Simmons Company
WILLIAM P. SIMMONS, Chairman
Southern Crate & Veneer Co.
DONALD B. SMILEY, Chairman
R. H. Macy & Co., Inc.
J. HENRY SMITH, Chairman
The Equitable Life Assurance Society
 of the United States
RAYMOND E. SNYDER
Senior Vice President
Merck & Co., Inc.
ELVIS J. STAHR, President
National Audubon Society
SYDNEY STEIN, JR., Partner
Stein Roe & Farnham
EDGAR B. STERN, JR., President
Royal Street Corporation
GEORGE A. STINSON, Chairman
National Steel Corporation
*WILLIAM C. STOLK, President
Government Research Corporation
ANNA LORD STRAUSS
New York, New York
ROBERT D. STUART, JR., President
Quaker Oats Company
REV. LEON H. SULLIVAN
Zion Baptist Church
JACKSON W. TARVER, President
Cox Enterprises, Inc.
WALTER N. THAYER, President
Whitney Communications Corporation
WAYNE E. THOMPSON
Senior Vice President
Dayton Hudson Corporation
CHARLES C. TILLINGHAST, JR., Chairman
Trans World Airlines, Inc.
HOWARD S. TURNER, Chairman
Turner Construction Company
L. S. TURNER, JR., President
Dallas Power & Light Co.
ALVIN W. VOGTLE, JR., President
The Southern Company, Inc.
LESLIE H. WARNER, Chairman
General Telephone & Electronics Corporation
ROBERT C. WEAVER
Department of Urban Affairs
Hunter College
SIDNEY J. WEINBERG, JR., Partner
Goldman, Sachs & Co.
HERMAN L. WEISS, Vice Chairman
General Electric Company
WILLIAM H. WENDEL, President
The Carborundum Company
JOHN H. WHEELER, President
Mechanics and Farmers Bank
GEORGE L. WILCOX
Vice Chairman, Corporate Affairs
Westinghouse Electric Corporation
*FRAZAR B. WILDE, Chairman Emeritus
Connecticut General Life Insurance Company
*W. WALTER WILLIAMS, Chairman
Continental, Inc.
MARGARET SCARBROUGH WILSON
President
Scarbroughs
WALTER W. WILSON, Partner
Morgan Stanley & Co.
ARTHUR M. WOOD, Chairman
Sears, Roebuck and Co.
THEODORE O. YNTEMA
Department of Economics
Oakland University

*Life Trustee

Honorary Trustees

CARL E. ALLEN
North Muskegon, Michigan
JAMES L. ALLEN, Honorary Chairman
Booz, Allen & Hamilton, Inc.
FRANK ALTSCHUL
New York, New York
S. CLARK BEISE
President (Retired)
Bank of America N.T. & S.A.
JOHN D. BIGGERS
Perrysburg, Ohio
WALTER R. BIMSON
Chairman Emeritus
Valley National Bank
ROGER M. BLOUGH
White & Case
FRED J. BORCH
New York, New York
THOMAS D. CABOT
Honorary Chairman of the Board
Cabot Corporation
EVERETT NEEDHAM CASE
Van Hornesville, New York
WALKER L. CISLER, Chairman
The Detroit Edison Company
JOHN L. COLLYER
Akron, Ohio
S. SLOAN COLT
New York, New York
JAMES B. CONANT
New York, New York
FAIRFAX M. CONE
Carmel, California
GARDNER COWLES
Chairman of the Board and
 Editorial Chairman
Cowles Communications, Inc.
JOHN P. CUNNINGHAM
Honorary Chairman of the Board
Cunningham & Walsh, Inc.
PAUL L. DAVIES, Senior Director
FMC Corporation
DONALD C. DAYTON, Director
Dayton Hudson Corporation
ROBERT W. ELSASSER
New Orleans, Louisiana
JAMES A. FARLEY, Chairman
The Coca-Cola Export Corporation
EDMUND FITZGERALD
Milwaukee, Wisconsin
WILLIAM C. FOSTER
Washington, D.C.
CLARENCE FRANCIS, Director
Economic Development Council of
 New York City, Inc.
ALFRED C. FULLER
West Hartford, Connecticut
PAUL S. GEROT
Honorary Chairman of the Board
The Pillsbury Company
MICHAEL L. HAIDER
New York, New York
J. V. HERD
Director
The Continental Insurance Companies
WILLIAM A. HEWITT, Chairman
Deere & Company
OVETA CULP HOBBY, Chairman
The Houston Post
HENRY R. JOHNSTON
Ponte Vedra Beach, Florida

THOMAS ROY JONES
Consultant, Schlumberger Limited
FREDERICK R. KAPPEL
Retired Chairman of the Board
American Telephone & Telegraph Company
DAVID M. KENNEDY
Northfield, Illinois
ROBERT J. KLEBERG, JR., President
King Ranch, Inc.
SIGURD S. LARMON
New York, New York
ROY E. LARSEN
Vice Chairman of the Board
Time Inc.
DAVID E. LILIENTHAL
President and Chairman
Development and Resources Corporation
ELMER L. LINDSETH
Shaker Heights, Ohio
JAMES A. LINEN
Chairman, Executive Committee
Time Inc.
GEORGE H. LOVE, Honorary Chairman
Consolidation Coal Company, Inc.
ROBERT A. LOVETT, Partner
Brown Brothers Harriman & Co.
ROY G. LUCKS
Del Monte Corporation
FRANKLIN J. LUNDING, Director
Jewel Companies, Inc.
L. F. McCOLLUM
Houston, Texas
JOHN A. McCONE
Los Angeles, California
FRANK L. MAGEE
Stahlstown, Pennsylvania
STANLEY MARCUS, Chairman
Neiman-Marcus Company
JOSEPH A. MARTINO
Honorary Chairman
N L Industries, Inc.
JOHN F. MERRIAM
San Francisco, California
LORIMER D. MILTON
Citizens Trust Company
DON G. MITCHELL
Summit, New Jersey
MALCOLM MUIR
Former Chairman and Editor-in-Chief
Newsweek
AKSEL NIELSEN
Chairman, Finance Committee
Ladd Petroleum Corporation
JAMES F. OATES, JR.
Sidley & Austin
W. A. PATTERSON, Retired Chairman
United Air Lines
EDWIN W. PAULEY, Chairman
Pauley Petroleum, Inc.
MORRIS B. PENDLETON
Vernon, California
DONALD C. POWER
Galloway, Ohio
M. J. RATHBONE
New York, New York
RAYMOND RUBICAM
Scottsdale, Arizona
GEORGE RUSSELL
Bloomfield Hills, Michigan
E. C. SAMMONS
Chairman of the Board (Emeritus)
United States National Bank of Oregon
NEIL D. SKINNER
Indianapolis, Indiana

ELLIS D. SLATER
Landrum, South Carolina

DONALD C. SLICHTER
Milwaukee, Wisconsin

S. ABBOT SMITH
Boston, Massachusetts

DAVIDSON SOMMERS, Consultant
The Equitable Life Assurance
 Society of the United States

PHILIP SPORN
New York, New York

ROBERT C. SPRAGUE
Honorary Chairman of the Board
Sprague Electric Company

ALLAN SPROUL
Kentfield, California

ROBERT G. SPROUL, President Emeritus
The University of California

FRANK STANTON, Consultant
Columbia Broadcasting System, Inc.

JOHN P. STEVENS, JR., Director
J. P. Stevens & Co., Inc.

ALEXANDER L. STOTT
Vice President and Comptroller
American Telephone & Telegraph Company

FRANK L. SULZBERGER
Chicago, Illinois

CHARLES P. TAFT
Cincinnati, Ohio

C. A. TATUM, JR., Chairman
Texas Utilities Company

ALAN H. TEMPLE
New York, New York

JAMES E. WEBB
Washington, D.C.

J. HUBER WETENHALL
New York, New York

WALTER H. WHEELER, JR.
Chairman, Executive Committee
Pitney-Bowes Inc.

A. L. WILLIAMS
Chairman, Finance Committee
IBM Corporation

HARRY W. ZINSMASTER, Chairman
Zinsmaster Baking Company

Trustees on Leave for Government Service

ROY L. ASH
Assistant to the President and Director of the
 Office of Management and Budget

FREDERICK B. DENT
Secretary of Commerce

DANIEL PARKER
Director at Large
Overseas Private Investment Corporation

CED Professional and Administrative Staff

ALFRED C. NEAL, *President*

ROBERT F. LENHART
*Vice President
for Research Administration*

FRANK W. SCHIFF
*Vice President
and Chief Economist*

S. CHARLES BLEICH
*Vice President for Finance
and Secretary, Board of Trustees*

SOL HURWITZ
*Vice President
and Director of Information*

GLENN R. PASCHALL
Director of Government Studies

ARNOLD H. PACKER
Senior Economist

ROBERT C. MEEHAN
*Deputy Treasurer
and Comptroller*

HARVEY M. LEWIS
PATRICIA M. O'CONNELL
Associate Directors, Finance

SEONG PARK
Economist

GEORGE F. FOWLER
*Director, Data Processing
and General Office Services*

CARL RIESER
Director of Publications

JOHN J. MALLEN, JR.
*Associate Director
of Information*

CLAUDIA PACKER
*Assistant Director
of Information*

MARY C. MUGIVAN
Publications Coordinator

GRACE CHAPPLE
Conference Manager

THEODORA BOSKOVIC
*Administrative Assistant
to President*

PUBLICATION ORDER FORM

To order CED publications please indicate number in column entitled "# Copies Desired." Then mail this order form and check for total amount in envelope to Distribution Division, CED, 477 Madison Ave., New York 10022.

ORDER NUMBER	STATEMENTS ON NATIONAL POLICY (paperbound)		# COPIES DESIRED

52P .. THE MANAGEMENT AND FINANCING OF COLLEGES — $1.50 _____
Proposes modern management techniques and innovative financing and student aid arrangements for public and private postsecondary education. Discusses goals, objectives, and accountability of these institutions, as well as faculty tenure, collective bargaining, and due process.

51P .. STRENGTHENING THE WORLD MONETARY SYSTEM — $1.50 _____
Recommends a program of basic reforms in the international monetary system, including the establishment of new rules to assure needed adjustments in currency exchange rates by both surplus and deficit countries.

50P .. FINANCING THE NATION'S HOUSING NEEDS — $1.50 _____
Examines the financal obstacles that hinder fulfillment of the nation's housing requirements and sets forth recommendations to make the nation's housing markets more responsive to the needs of all sectors of society.

49P .. BUILDING A NATIONAL HEALTH-CARE SYSTEM — $1.75 _____
Sets forth a plan for the organization, management, and financing of a national health care system which would improve the delivery of health care services while extending insurance coverage to all Americans.

48P .. A NEW TRADE POLICY TOWARD COMMUNIST COUNTRIES — $1.50 _____
Recommends a continued easing of U.S. trade and credit restrictions against communist countries, bringing them in line with U.S. policies toward other industrialized nations.

47P .. HIGH EMPLOYMENT WITHOUT INFLATION: A POSITIVE PROGRAM FOR ECONOMIC STABILIZATION — $1.50 _____
Recommends a continued governmnetal role in wage-price policies, calls for basic structural changes in the economy, and urges an incentive system of decontrol. Emphasizes that fiscal and monetary policies must remain the key element of the nation's economic efforts.

46P .. REDUCING CRIME AND ASSURING JUSTICE — $1.50 _____
An integrated examination of needed reforms in the entire system of criminal justice, including courts, prosecution, police, and corrections.

45P .. MILITARY MANPOWER AND NATIONAL SECURITY — $1.00 _____
Focuses on several critical issues relating to military manpower.

44P .. THE UNITED STATES AND THE EUROPEAN COMMUNITY — $1.50 _____
Deals with the development of the Common Market into an enlarged European Economic Community and its potential effects on Western European trade, investment, and monetary relations with the U.S. and other free-world nations. Recommends immediate steps to halt deterioration in the world trading system.

43P .. IMPROVING FEDERAL PROGRAM PERFORMANCE — $1.50 _____
Focuses attention on three major areas of concern about federal programs: (1) the choice of policy goals and program objectives, (2) the selection of programs that will achieve those objectives, and (3) the execution of the programs and the evaluation of their performance.

42P .. SOCIAL RESPONSIBILITIES OF BUSINESS CORPORATIONS — $1.50 _____
Develops a rationale for corporate involvement in solving such pressing social problems as urban blight, poverty, and pollution. Examines the need for the corporation to make its social responsibilities an integral part of its business objectives. Points out at the same time the proper limitations on such activities.

41P .. EDUCATION FOR THE URBAN DISADVANTAGED: From Preschool to Employment $1.50 _____
A comprehensive review of the current state of education for disadvantaged minorities; sets forth philosophical and operational principles which are imperative if the mission of the urban schools is to be accomplished successfully.

40P .. FURTHER WEAPONS AGAINST INFLATION — $1.50 _____
Examines the problem of reconciling high employment and price stability. Maintains that measures to supplement general fiscal and monetary policies will be needed—including the use of voluntary wage-price (or "incomes") policies, as well as measures to change the structural and institutional environment in which demand policy operates.

39P .. MAKING CONGRESS MORE EFFECTIVE — $1.00 _____
Points out the structural and procedural handicaps limiting the ability of Congress to respond to the nation's needs. Proposes a far-reaching Congressional reform program.

38P .. DEVELOPMENT ASSISTANCE TO SOUTHEAST ASIA — $1.50 _____
Deals with the importance of external resources—financial, managerial, and technological, including public and private—to the development of Southeast Asia.

37P .. TRAINING AND JOBS FOR THE URBAN POOR — $1.25 _____
Explores ways of abating poverty that arises from low wages and chronic unemployment or underemployment. Evaluates current manpower training and employment efforts by government and business.

SEE OTHER SIDE→

ORDER NUMBER		# COPIES DESIRED
36P .. IMPROVING THE PUBLIC WELFARE SYSTEM	$1.50	_____

Analyzes the national problem of poverty and the role played by the present welfare system. The statement recommends major changes in both the rationale and the administration of the public assistance program, with a view to establishing need as the sole criterion for coverage.

35P .. RESHAPING GOVERNMENT IN METROPOLITAN AREAS	$1.00	_____

Recommends a two-level system of government for metropolitan areas: an area-wide level and a local level comprised of "community districts."

34P .. ASSISTING DEVELOPMENT IN LOW-INCOME COUNTRIES	$1.25	_____

Offers a sound rationale for public support of the U.S. economic assistance program and recommends a far-ranging set of priorities for U.S. Government policy.

33P .. NONTARIFF DISTORTIONS OF TRADE	$1.00	_____

Examines the complex problem of dealing with nontariff distortions of trade arising from governmental measures that create special barriers to imports and incentives to exports.

32P .. FISCAL AND MONETARY POLICIES FOR STEADY ECONOMIC GROWTH	$1.00	_____

Reexamines the role of fiscal and monetary policies in achieving the basic economic objectives of high employment, price stability, economic growth, and equilibrium in the nation's international payments.

31P .. FINANCING A BETTER ELECTION SYSTEM	$1.00	_____

Urges comprehensive modernization of election and campaign procedures at national, state, and local levels. Proposes ways to reduce costs and spread them more widely through tax credits.

30P .. INNOVATION IN EDUCATION: New Directions for the American School	$1.00	_____
28P .. MODERNIZING STATE GOVERNMENT	$1.00	_____
27P .. TRADE POLICY TOWARD LOW-INCOME COUNTRIES	$1.50	_____
24P .. HOW LOW INCOME COUNTRIES CAN ADVANCE THEIR OWN GROWTH	$1.50	_____
23P .. MODERNIZING LOCAL GOVERNMENT	$1.00	_____
22P .. A BETTER BALANCE IN FEDERAL TAXES ON BUSINESS	75¢	_____
21P .. BUDGETING FOR NATIONAL OBJECTIVES	$1.00	_____
15P .. EDUCATING TOMORROW'S MANAGERS	$1.00	_____
14P .. IMPROVING EXECUTIVE MANAGEMENT IN THE FEDERAL GOVERNMENT	$1.50	_____
9P .. ECONOMIC LITERACY FOR AMERICANS	75¢	_____
1P .. ECONOMIC GROWTH IN THE UNITED STATES	$1.00	_____

Quantity discounts: 10-24 copies—10%, 25-49 copies—15%, 50-99 copies—20%, 100-249 copies—30%

NOTE TO EDUCATORS: Instructors in colleges and universities may obtain up to 5 free copies of those CED Statements on National Policy which they intend to use in courses they are teaching. **Please mention the course name when ordering.** For more than 5 copies, an educational discount of 20% will apply.

Course ....

☐ I am enclosing $ .... for the copies ordered above.

☐ Please bill me. *(Payment must accompany orders under $10.00)*

DO YOU WANT ALL CED PUBLICATIONS WHEN ISSUED?

☐ I would like to obtain all CED publications as soon as they are issued. Please send me information about the CED Reader Forum subscription plan.

☐ Please send me newest list of publications.

Name ....

Organization ....

Address ....

City .... State .... Zip ....

☐ Businessman ☐ Educator ☐ Professional